The Modern Voice in American Poetry

William Doreski

The Modern Voice in
American Poetry

University Press of Florida
Gainesville/Tallahassee/Tampa/Boca Raton
Pensacola/Orlando/Miami/Jacksonville

Copyright 1995 by the Board of Regents of the State of Florida
Printed in the United States of America on acid-free paper ∞

00 99 98 97 96 95 6 5 4 3 2 1

Library of Congress Cataloging-in-Publication Data

Doreski, William
The modern voice in American poetry / William Doreski.
p.   cm.
Includes bibliographical references (p.) and index.
ISBN 0-8130-1362-3
1. American poetry—20th century—History and criticism. 2. Modernism
(Literature)—United States. I. Title.
PS310.M57D67 1995
811' .509—dc20   94-48343

The University Press of Florida is the scholarly publishing agency for the State
University System of Florida, comprised of Florida A & M University, Florida
Atlantic University, Florida International University, Florida State University,
University of Central Florida, University of Florida, University of North
Florida, University of South Florida, and University of West Florida.

University Press of Florida
15 Northwest 15th Street
Gainesville, FL 32611

In Memory of Dr. Henry Vincent Grattan

He brushed away the thunder, then the clouds,
Then the colossal illusion of heaven. Yet still
The sky was blue. He wanted imperceptible air.
He wanted to see. He wanted the eye to see
And not be touched by blue. He wanted to know,
A naked man who regarded himself in the glass
Of air, who looked for the world beneath the blue,
Without blue, without any turquoise tint or phase,
Any azure under-side or after-color.

Wallace Stevens, "Landscape with Boat"

Contents

Preface

Issues of voice and related rhetoric problems have shaped discussions of poetry since the era of Coleridge and Wordsworth. Major innovations in genre, especially the development of the historically informed dramatic monologue and various dialogic modes, offered fresh opportunities for poets of the late Victorian and early modernist periods, so that much of the history of modern poetry—as Herbert F. Tucker summarizes it in his essay "Dramatic Monologue and the Overhearing of Lyric"—is the incorporation of history and the intrusion of narrative and dramatic impurities into the meditative and lyric voices. Or, as Tilottama Rajan puts it in discussing the earlier romantics, "Lyric is increasingly absorbed into larger structures which place it within a world of difference" (195). The major modernist poets—Eliot, Yeats, Stevens, and Pound—as well as first-generation postmodernists like Lowell and Berryman, recapitulate the process by rediscovering lyric in their early work, then learning to "exploit the internal otherness of the dramatic monologue" and, in the case of Lowell at least, overcoming subjectivity even in frankly autobiographical writing by generating for the personal voice a privileged historical perspective (Tucker, 239). As Tucker describes the process, "When the lyric bubble burst within its bell jar, poetry became modern once again in its return to the historically responsive and dialogic mode that Browning, Tennyson, and others had brought forward from the Romantics" (239).

The desire for purity in lyric, as it still occasionally arises, seems regressive, and historical and dialogic modes of discourse have almost universally shaped the important poetry of the mid-nineteenth century and that written since World War I. The fiction of the dissociated speaker, devised by the New Critics to historicize and dramatize every poem, even the most intimate lyric, as Tucker argues, answered both to pedagogical needs and to a need to demystify the subjective mode that had focused readers of poetry exclusively on feeling rather than understanding. That critical fiction has received fresh life in recent linguistic theories, which emphasize the arbitrary, uncontrollable complexity of language, and the tendency, therefore, of texts to dissociate themselves from their authors. In "What Is an Author?" and "The Death of the Author" Michel Foucault and Roland Barthes suggest that the very concept of authorship is socially suspect and largely irrelevant; but rather than being widely accepted, this extreme dissociation of text from author has sparked reconsideration of the role of authorship and of the cultural and social context of writing.

This book operates in the area defined by the critical concerns and fictions centered on issues of voice, rhetoric, interiority (imagination) and exteriority (landscape), and history. It is not the "semiotics of genre" that Rajan argues we need, but it is a step in that direction. My purpose is not to resolve the large theoretical issues involved: such a resolution would be suspect because poetry resists totalizing or universalizing theories, and because certain issues probably cannot be resolved in our current cultural framework. Even obvious but doubtful binary oppositions— self and other, subject and object—are so ingrained in the texture of our culture and language that although resolved in the momentary transcendence of certain poems, they nonetheless regain their privileged status as soon as the critic names them—even if the purpose of that naming is to problematize or deconstruct the opposition. Criticism lacks the spatial dimension that distinguishes poetry from other modes of discourse. No other use of language seems as three-dimensional as poetry because no other mode of discourse so manipulates both the page and the listening ear as sites of spatial contention. Fiction, too, has an important spatial dimension, as Joseph Frank has demonstrated, but the function of verse is to mobilize even more resources and generate an illusion of dimension comparable, in some respects, to perspective in painting or the solid closure of sculpture.

However, the spatial dimension of verse requires for full exploration another book with a larger scope and more capacious critical outlook. My purpose here is merely to offer some practical applications of contemporary concerns in the study of rhetorical issues in poetry, not to cover every possible sort of problem, and especially not to offer a complete semiotic of lyric or the monologue. While no overarching or totalizing thesis links these discussions, at least two premises underlie their arguments. First, the modernist poets, in their efforts to escape the stifling desire for lyric purity renewed in the late nineteenth century and to return to the more interdiscursive lyric, monologic, and dialogic forms of the romantics, turned to prose fiction, the drama, and extraliterary sources to expand the rhetorical range of their poetics. The modernists welcomed symbolist urban topics and colloquial diction, but their suspicion of the mystifying power of symbolism, their sense of the dialogic nature of language, and their embrace of the lyric narrative (like Rimbaud's "Le bateau ivre") and other impure genres (such as the one described by M.H. Abrams as the greater Romantic lyric) shaped a new kind of poetic.

The modernist poets experienced a vast shift in the relationship between poetry and society. They followed Baudelaire in noting that the industrial-bourgeois world was not the same world that engendered Shakespeare and Racine, and to complete their educations they suffered the cultural and social brutalization of two world wars. Even Eliot, with his enormous regard for a selectively defined tradition, in his earliest poetry demonstrated an awareness of the new political implications of a bourgeois society caught in culture shock. Unfortunately, for Pound and Eliot this awareness became oppressive, and their unease with the deterioration of accepted cultural standards eventually led them to authoritarian positions and allegiances.

For Frost, Stevens, and Williams, who resisted the draw of Europe, the problem was to invent a rhetoric comprehensive enough to meet the challenge posed by Whitman of inventing a poetic voice to fill the vast American landscape. Frost accepted the task by substantially expanding the available range of the dramatic monologue and dialogue, by adopting blank verse to the American idiom (and vice versa), and by refining the interior monologue to reflect the interior lives of ahistorical Americans confronting the shabby remains of the wilderness and their Jeffersonian agrarian dream. Stevens went further, believing that the poet's task was to define a whole new relationship among the imagination, reality, and poetry. He argued that America presented both the need and the opportunity for a fresh mythology, a new supreme fiction that would define the landscape of the American imagination in a rhetoric and imagery untainted by the decay of European tradition. Stevens did not propose to do away with mythology, religion, and tradition but to reinvent them, if necessary, in the stark landscapes of Connecticut or Pennsylvania, where new mythologies, if properly nourished, might thrive. Williams, with his matter-of-fact attitude and scientific education, took a phenomenological approach to abstraction and a pragmatic-materialist approach to language. Their relationship, he felt, had to be grounded in immediacy not tradition. History required skepticism; and facts, while a respectable source of ideas, also were limited and could not be made to transcend themselves. The proper language of poetry would be present tense, concrete, inspirited with desire, and tempered with perception. The language had to be idiomatic, immensely compressed, and as nonmetrical in its rhythms as possible. Stevens also wrestled with the problem of rhythm and subtly undermined blank verse by writing poems that on the page resemble regular pentameter but refuse (cleverly and quite rhythmically) to scan. Williams often fractured his poems on the page so that their form reflected their rhetorical drive. He embraced the public and political rhetoric of persuasion, the ordinary speech of the streets, the urgent discourse of the reformer, and the bemused meditative voice of his novels and short stories of social commentary. Most startlingly, many of his poems—most notably *Paterson*—make a collage of contrasting rhetorical strategies and levels of diction, shattering the tonal consistency that marked the lyric poetry of the late nineteenth century, and instead embracing a sometimes irrational exuberance. With Marianne Moore, a poet he otherwise could hardly less resemble, he shared a passion for found speech, the unmediated rhetorical effect.

Robert Lowell, however literary history will judge him, seems an important transitional figure and a central reinterpreter of the modernist poetic idiom. His aesthetic looks back to Eliot and Crane and forward to Plath, Snodgrass, Rich, and Ginsberg. His rhetorical strategies are complex enough to require a book-length study, but here it will suffice to note that his further development of the interior monologue, working

from the nineteenth-century models and the examples of the first generation of modernists, reached into new territory, into psychological realms
largely undescribed before Freud drew our attention to them. The earlier
modernists recognized how Baudelaire (following Poe), Browning, and
Henry James had anticipated Freud, and in poems like *Hugh Selwyn
Mauberley* and "Portrait of a Lady" reinvented English poetry in the light
of those complex delvings into the interior. Lowell, by way of Eliot and
Hart Crane, reinvents Baudelaire's urban imagery in terms of twentieth-
century Boston, but, more significantly, with *Life Studies* he reread the
formalism Eliot had retained at the center of the English tradition as he
understood it, and adapted to it the iconoclastic, colloquial rhetorical
strategies of Williams, bringing to his technique a stronger sense of the
arbitrary and sometimes puzzling relationship between language and the
interior world and a more subtle rhetorical sense than Williams's. In a
way, Lowell followed Eliot in turning symbolism inside out. The sym-
bolists embraced the image as logos, honoring its immutable link to the
ineffable. Rather than using language as a means to transcend the exterior world, the great otherness, Lowell follows one aspect of the poetics
of Eliot and Crane in turning language inward, rejecting the signifier/
signified relationship by using language to interiorize the world and demonstrate how perception and imagination through language revise the
exterior in terms of the poet's presence. Yet Lowell acknowledges a tension between lyric interiority and dramatic-narrative dialectical exteriority.
His most distinctive rhetorical achievement—the formulation of the trope
of vulnerability—encapsulates the rhetoric of the interior; but his linking of psychological and public concerns in poetry that is both political
and personal remains his most distinguished achievement.

This leads to my second premise, that the modernist poem exposes
a conflict between a responsibility to history, tradition, or society, and
the poet's desire to generate what Frank Lentricchia describes as "an ideal
integrated consciousness," a world of the poet's own making (1975, 109).
Williams, for example, is torn between the attractions of history, which
he views with deep mistrust, and the dream life he values but which is
too unsubstantial to generate the kind of language his poetry requires.
The modernist period is an extension of the romantic era in which, as
Rajan says, "lyric is increasingly absorbed into larger structures which
place it within a world of differences" (195). This relationship between

lyric and "larger structure" and the "larger world of differences" thus invoked is an important topic of this book.

My discussion is informed, I hope, by years of reading and teaching modern and contemporary literary theory, but I do not adhere to any particular set of dogmas, nor have I found such adherence in the work of others especially productive. The list of cited works at the end of this book exposes some of my indebtedness, but I would like to mention a few critics and books that in a more general way have aided me. Despite the recently raised political issues, every contemporary student of theory and poetry owes much to Paul de Man, particularly for his essential essay "The Allegory of Temporality," as well as the other important essays in *Blindness and Insight*. The collection *Lyric Poetry: Beyond New Criticism,* edited by Chaviva Hošek and Patricia Parker, contains many important essays, including those by Tucker and Rajan cited above, and Mary Jacobus's "Apostrophe and Lyric Voice in the *Prelude,*" which engages the problem of voice as a rhetorical function at a profound level. Among the many other critics who have taught me much over the years, four loom large. Helen Vendler instructed me in the pitch and tone of poetic voice and to understand it as a function of the poet's language, while the forceful writings of Randall Jarrell alerted me to the importance of the poetry of one's own era. Marjorie Perloff, in her wide-ranging essays, offers a model of critical flexibility and undogmatic generosity; and the various pioneering studies of modern poets by A. Walton Litz have demonstrated how fresh and inexhaustible, after decades of critical study, these poets remain.

Acknowledgments

Thanks and acknowledgment are given to New Directions Publishing Corporation for permission to quote from the following works: *Personae,* by Ezra Pound, copyright 1926, 1931, 1971 by Ezra Pound; and *The Collected Poems of William Carlos Williams,* volume 1, copyright 1938 New Directions, and 1986 by A. Walton Litz and Christopher MacGowan.

Ecco Press has granted permission to reprint the following poems: "Gretel in Darkness," copyright 1971, 1972, 1973, 1974 by Louise Glück, from *The House on Marshland,* by Louise Glück; "Snow," copyright 1990 by Louise Glück, from *Ararat,* by Louise Glück; and "On an East Wind from the Wars," copyright 1961, 1962, 1968, 1972, 1973, 1974, 1983 by

Alan Dugan, from *New and Collected Poems 1961–1983,* by Alan Dugan.

Excerpts from *Life Studies, The Dolphin,* and *Day by Day,* by Robert Lowell, copyright 1959, 1973, 1977 by Robert Lowell, are reprinted with permission of Farrar, Straus, and Giroux.

Excerpts from T.S. Eliot, "Portrait of a Lady," from *Collected Poems 1909–1962* by T.S. Eliot, copyright 1934, 1963, by T.S. Eliot, are reprinted with permission of Harcourt, Brace.

Excerpts from *The Complete Poetry of Robert Frost,* copyright 1971 by Lesley Frost Ballantine, are reprinted with the permission of Holt, Rinehart and Winston.

Alfred A. Knopf has granted permission to reprint excerpts from *Collected Poems,* by Wallace Stevens, copyright 1954 by Wallace Stevens.

W.W. Norton has granted permission to reprint excerpts from "Easter Morning," copyright 1981 by A.R. Ammons, from *A Coast of Trees,* by A.R. Ammons.

Princeton University Press has granted permission to reprint "Long Branch, New Jersey," from *Sadness and Happiness,* by Robert Pinsky, copyright 1975 by Robert Pinsky.

Viking Press has granted permission to reprint lines from *April Galleons,* by John Ashbery, copyright 1984, 1985, 1986, 1987 by John Ashbery. Excerpts from *A Wave,* by John Ashbery, copyright 1984 by John Ashbery, are reprinted with permission.

Early versions of portions of chapters 1, 2, and 5 appeared in *Ariel, Twentieth-Century Literature,* and *Arizona Quarterly;* many thanks to the editors of these journals.

I am deeply grateful to A. Walton Litz, Walter Sutton, and James Longenbach, who read and commented on this manuscript, and especially to Carole Doreski for both scholarly and personal support. I am also grateful to the staffs of the Firestone Library of Princeton University, the Houghton Library of Harvard University, and the Mason Library of Keene State College for their assistance.

A Note on References

Parenthetic notations in the text refer, by page and often by date or author, to sources listed as works cited at the end of this volume. Thus a parenthetical notation following several lines quoted from a Wallace Stevens poem might read (1954, 225), while the corresponding entry in works cited would be: Stevens, Wallace. 1954. *Collected Poems.* New York: Alfred A. Knopf.

If an author's name does not appear in the text I have placed it in the parenthetical notation, as (Bush, 288), or (Stevens 1951, 25). If the author and source are mentioned in the text, or if only one work by a named author appears in works cited, the parenthetical notation will contain only a page number.

To avoid cluttering the text I have noted the source of each poem only once, following my first quotation from it.

Frost

Lyric Monologue and Landscape

In "Education by Poetry," published in the *Amherst Graduates' Quarterly* in 1931, Robert Frost invoked the intricacies, including the limits, of metaphor as knowledge. "All metaphor breaks down somewhere. . . . That is the beauty of it. It is touch and go with the metaphor, and until you have lived with it long enough you don't know when it is going" (1966, 41). By that time Frost had "lived with" metaphor through many books. His early poems, which he had collected and published sixteen years before, had displayed a sophisticated sense of the limits of metaphor, a careful testing of allegorical possibilities, and an inclination to expand narrative models through rhetorical motifs other than those already enshrined in lyric conventions.

The best of the poems Frost would write in the following two decades would go further by making rhetorical self-critique an intrinsic structural and thematic element of their poetics. Further, he would embody this rhetorical exploration and commentary in poems where rural or wilderness landscapes occupy significant roles in which nature, scarred by human use and abuse, functions as a trope of otherness, repelling the poet's dogged queries and offering, instead of response, a mute rhetoric of nonhuman forms. This enables his speakers to define themselves through their interrogation of the world, finding in their own querulousness a quality that is peculiarly human.

This discussion will first examine the way Frost develops meditative self-awareness as the basis for the critical speaking voice of some of his lyric monologues, and then will consider how in a landscape poem, indebted in some ways to eighteenth-century vista poems, Frost unfolds his scenery phenomenologically, using the trope of otherness to illuminate the speaking self. I hope also to suggest how Frost's vast rhetorical resources, possibly the most impressive of any poet in this century, serve an intellectual and poetic intelligence of deep skepticism, profound self-aware-ness, and a grasp of the alien quality of nature unmatched by any poet since Dickinson.

"The Wood-Pile," "After Apple-Picking," and "Directive"

"The Wood-Pile" and "After Apple-Picking," both from *North of Boston* (1914), illustrate the two poles of a language of meditation drawn, re-spectively, from Dante and the tradition of allegorical landscape, and from Wordsworth and the romantic acknowledgment of the otherness of land-scape. Each poem confronts comparable problems in signification: the limits of allegory (a walk in winter woods, a journey over a rutted coun-try road), the unruly complexity of the symbol (the woodpile, the Grail), and the loss of religious faith and iconography and the difficulty of find-ing a comparably significant but secular language. These problems signal an apparent exhaustion of lyric conventions and encourage Frost to use his characteristic irony to deconstruct the meditative voice, expose it as a fiction, and renew the lyric sense of wonder and discovery by invoking a speech-oriented language (a dialogic rather than monologic voice) more informal, less conventionally poetic, and more intimate than the lan-guage it displaces. That is, the renewal proceeds by visibly displacing one language model for another. Frost, unlike Williams, for example, does not refuse established lyric models, but escapes the conventional language of meditation, monologue, and lyric ecstasy without entirely abandoning established formal paradigms.

I will examine these two poems to trace the process of confronting, bracketing, and refusing the same conventional modes of meditation (al-legory, symbolism) they initially invoke, their critique or establishment of the limits of these modes, and their turn toward renewal through alter-nate language modes. I will then consider how "Directive," as a paradigm of Frost's later poetics, draws upon a more integrated model of medita-tion that evokes neither allegory nor symbol as a mystifying function. From the start this poem poses the dialogic mode as an alternative to the earlier monologues. In "Directive" the speaker's imagination (which Bakhtin would recognize here as self-consciously dialogic) posits an on-going critique of its own processes as a proper meditative model.

"The Wood-Pile" opens by invoking Dante's motif of the lost soul, the wanderer in the dark wood. The speaker warns us that like many other allegorical landscapes this one is no place in particular and cannot be readily named, too formal with its "view . . . all in lines / Straight up and down of tall slim trees / Too much alike to mark or name a place by." Such places, lacking adequately differed signifiers, typically entrap the traveler, and the reader might well expect this speaker to fall prey to self-doubts, misgivings of the sort that suggest that inner and outer landscapes are actually one. Frost's wood is frozen, gray, and snowy, and by lacking clear definition it threatens the absorption or erasure of the self.

The speaker is neither passive nor desperate. He offers no particular moral dilemma, displays no fear, and asserts a role in his own salvation by positing the choice between turning back and going on. No white leopard—a figure clearly not of the waking world—leads him on, though another natural emblem, an otherwise undistinguished "small bird" flies before him, neither leading him nor quite fleeing from him, as if it toyed with its own allegorical role but cannot quite fulfill it. The speaker implies, in his playful, uncommitted personification of the bird, that this bird's reluctance to name itself derives from its reluctance to expose its inner life, which centers, for the moment, on fear. The speaker assumes that the bird believes it is being chased for its feather, its metonymic self, "like one who takes / Everything said as personal to himself." One can conceive of someone foolish enough to take all landscapes, allegorical or otherwise, as personal to himself; but this Wordsworthian position does not suit Frost, and his refusal of this relatively simple link between being and nature redirects the poem from allegory to a less conventionally predicated mode.

By invoking the convention of the allegorical landscape, Frost suggests the possibility of constructing his poem entirely within a structural certainty in which every motif, every emblem finds a place and contributes toward the reconciliation of self and other. But Frost has a delicate sense of scale. Dante's immensely complex poem accomplishes its task only by invoking the entire structure of medieval Catholic theology and shaping it to the even more inclusive convention of landscape allegory. Frost, who always insisted that the play of language is central to poetry, loves to tease the reader by setting up expectations of grandeur that if actually attempted in so brief and colloquial a poem would surely fail.

"The Wood-Pile" turns abruptly, takes "One flight out sideways," as it were, and forgets its allegorical beginnings as the speaker forgets the bird and lets "his little fear / Carry him off the way I might have gone." The bird delves further into the allegorical landscape, but the speaker, alerted by his discovery, enters a new mode.

As some versions of literary history would have it, poetry altered its course in the romantic era by positing the symbol as a logocentric repository of meaning outside of language. "The Wood-Pile" somewhat wryly critiques that version of literary history, and in addition critiques both the convention the poem first invokes then abandons and the newer convention it turns to and gently mocks. Paul de Man notes that the earlier romantics resisted the temptation to collapse being and the natural object into a single entity or sign (15). Wordsworth toyed with the idea that in place of a firm grounding of faith, imagination, by means of a self-reflexive poetic language, might empower the linguistic sign with the presence of nature. But he well understood the paradoxical quality of his endeavor, and the *Prelude* displays his awareness of the negating power as well as the nostalgia of the imagination.

In "The Wood-Pile," at the very moment of empowerment, Frost undercuts the utility of the woodpile as a symbol of human presence by recalling that, like all signifiers, it has something of allegory in it—in this instance the bird, which "went behind it [the woodpile] to make his last stand" (1969, 101). He also reminds us that the symbol, unlike the allegorical emblem, embodies rather than merely suggests its own history. Though isolated in its human import, the woodpile is the monolith that represents all history, all endeavor, all made things, and is, therefore, "older sure than this year's cutting, / Or even last year's or the year's before." Yet isolate, human-made, and symbolic though it is, the woodpile lacks stability, and is losing its own sense of origin by returning to nature and surrendering its logocentric status. Already "Clematis / Had wound strings round and round it like a bundle," reclaiming it as the bark warps off and the wood deconstructs into its natural state. This disintegrative process generates the tropes of impoverishment Richard Poirier finds in this poem (140). The woodpile, claimed from nature and therefore claimed by Being, is slowly reverting to a simpler form of sign, returning to the world of allegory, in de Man's sense, in which the primal and ethical distinction between the mind and the world is relatively clearly defined, but in which metaphor, deprived of a central shaping role, seems impoverished.

Frost's paradoxical moralism—which argues that "only / Someone who lived in turning to fresh tasks / Could so forget his handiwork on which / He spent himself, the labor of his ax"—both conceals and reveals the gap between being and nature by calling into question the very process of making and naming. What is the use of doing tasks at all if one spends oneself only to abandon and forget the results of one's labor? The answer is the poem's critique of its own process of hacking a symbol—the woodpile—from conventional allegorical motifs. In concealing its refusal to cross the gulf between sign and nature, this symbolic decaying woodpile exposes its—and the poem's—self-deconstruction. The woodpile completes the failure of signification by refusing to warm its author, instead warming "as best it could" the original allegorical landscape, which it seems to endow momentarily with a human presence.

The consequence of this shift from allegory to symbol is to suggest that neither language mode is sufficient to engender a poetic sufficient to overcome the nostalgia for the human world, the primacy of the external object. "The Wood-Pile" is a poem about the search for origins and the limitations of the most obvious attempts to reconcile nature and the mind. It is also a poem about the power of language to invoke the very idea of presence, an idea that if not realized in fact is capable of generating imagery that is so evocative as to demonstrate that metaphor-generated illusion can as generously engage the sensuous being as the actual presence of the evoked object. The opening line "Out walking in the frozen swamp one gray day" signals a pattern of open vowel sounds that corresponds to the open view through the leafless trees. The imagery, including the closing picture of the woodpile decaying in the middle of the swamp, corresponds to a sense of expanding possibilities. The forgetfulness of the woodcutter corresponds, the speaker believes, to a larger sense of purpose. Renewal through language, then, is not the property of particular language-models (allegory or symbol) but a larger argument shaped by and around their limitations. By exploiting and conflating lyric conventions rather than attempting to abandon them, Frost argues from their relationship; in miniaturizing a literary-historical model (the displacement of allegory by symbolism) he replicates the expansive history of the attempt to resolve through language and imagination the isolation of the mind. In doing so, he implicitly argues that the positing of fictional modes of representation affirms the practical utility of the language of imagery to engage the senses and sustain at least a momentary illusion of natural or human presence.

"After Apple-Picking," with its irregular meter and rhyme scheme (described by Reuben Brower, 24–25) and its dreamy, almost surreal atmosphere, is in some ways uncharacteristic of Frost. In acceding to the proposal, in Poirier's words, that "only labor can penetrate to the essential facts of natural life," the speaker invokes and then, after achieving a degree of satiation, refuses the iconographic status of the apple as repository of the plenitude of desire. Though the apparatus for engaging this symbol (his "two-pointed ladder," a metaphor of metaphor, as Poirier points out [295]) remains in place "sticking through a tree / Toward heaven still," the speaker has exhausted through satiation his passion for everything the apple has represented, its entire history as a signifier. But because the speaker has already indulged himself, because he admits he "desired" the "great harvest," the poem has to acknowledge fully the illusion of totality the apple (and the very concept of symbolism) embodies before freeing itself from that no longer satisfactory goal.

In reviewing and finally rejecting the totalization represented by apple picking, the speaker has to invoke and face the possibility that without the totalizing synthesis of the symbol consciousness itself might depart and leave him in a state too uncertain to name. It would be sleep, but whether sleep could function as a metaphor of death or whether it would be death itself he cannot say. The difficulty occurs early in the poem, when the speaker, immediately upon recognizing that the apple icon is losing its grip on him ("I am done with apple-picking now") begins "drowsing off." This is not ordinary exhaustion, but, he explains, is linked to a shift in vision, a new way of looking at the world:

> I cannot rub the strangeness from my sight
> I got from looking through a pane of glass
> I skimmed this morning from the drinking trough
> And held against the world of hoary grass. (1969, 68)

That is, he holds against (both in the sense of comparison and of bearing a grudge) the "world of hoary grass" the very possibility of a fresher way of seeing, an unconventional poetics. But he cannot sustain it: the satiation of the apple-world of symbol, determinate meaning, and unquenchable desire was heavy upon him this morning, and he "let it fall and break."

Nevertheless, he had already, before the day had fully started, determined to refuse the illusionary desire, regardless of consequences. Therefore, later in the day, although exhausted, he retains the sense of strangeness. Sleep, postulated before he dropped the pane of ice glass, brings upon him a still more fully saturated vision of apples. This vision compels him to face the materiality of the apple, "every fleck of russet," to suggest not so much its actuality but the futility of the totalizing desire that induced the "great harvest" with its "rumbling sound / Of load on load of apples coming in." The vision of apples thus invokes an incoherent, disarticulate language of desire mocking itself and him.

The consequences of surrender to symbolic desire are both physical and metaphysical. The former is relatively mild—"My instep arch not only keeps the ache, / It keeps the pressure of a ladder-round." The sense-impressions linger with relatively little pain, but the psychic drift from investment in the symbol to satiation and loss of faith is the center of strangeness in the poem and has potentially dire implications. If, as Poirier argues, "the penetrating power of labor can be evinced in 'apple-picking' or in writing or reading about it, and any one of these activities brings us close to seeing how apples and all that surround them can be symbolic of the spirit," then to admit to having had "too much / Of apple-picking" is not to deny the spirit but to refuse the necessity or the efficacy of the symbol (294). It is also to question, agnostically, whether the symbol can effectively link the ineffable to this world. The speaker now doubts the earlier promise of fulfillment, a kind of pact between himself and the apple crop. He concedes that the gap between consciousness and object is intolerable, and that his desires, too, because external and illusory, conceal the psychological and linguistic inadequacies of his investment in the apple as signifier. As Poirier argues, "the intensity of labor has brought him in touch with a vocabulary of 'apples,' 'trees,' 'scent,' 'ladders,' 'harvests,' of ascents and descents that make it impossible for him not to say one thing in terms of another" (298); but this conscious recognition of the necessity of metaphor only generates an exhausting self-consciousness. The vision of a new poetics, glimpsed briefly that morning, has only confirmed the speaker's sense that the physical world has failed to embody itself in the symbols his consciousness has attempted to possess.

Not even "ten thousand thousand fruit to touch" can provide enough sense-impression to overcome this growing drowsiness, this feeling of loss. Yet in refusing the iconic potency of the apple symbol the speaker has opened himself to a new poetic, and with it a growing awareness of the fragility of the physical world. The apples, after all, are only so much pulp:

> For all
> That struck the earth,
> No matter if not bruised or spiked with stubble,
> Went surely to the cider-apple heap
> As of no worth.

However, the failure of apples to maintain their formal value under slightly altered conditions suggests to the speaker his own status as formal construct, which his refusal of symbolic desire has called into question. When he says he "can see what will trouble / This sleep" of his, "whatever sleep it is," he reminds us that by deconstructing his symbolic desire he has called into question the very nature of consciousness and being. The woodchuck that, if present, "could say whether it's [the speaker's sleep] like his" is absent primarily in the sense that everything else is absent: not an actual component of the sign, the very nature of which has been exposed here. The difference between the woodchuck's "Long sleep" and "just some human sleep" is that the animal, without the gift and curse of language, has no measure for his sleep, no desire (even to wake), nothing but the negation of his vision of harvest. The speaker of the poem, on the other hand, cannot say whether he, too, will retain his sense of loss, his absence of desire, and his awareness of the illusory nature of the symbol, or whether he will revert to the desire-burdened state of "human sleep" (the previously established form of which is "winter sleep" informed by "the scent of apples"), whatever its metaphorical consequences.

The exhaustion of the romantic-lyric convention of the symbol finds its consequence where it begins: in the speaker's awareness, or lack of awareness, of his own state of being. By displacing the language model of the symbol with only a fleeting glimpse (through a sheet of ice, a most tentative form of matter) of an alternate linguistic or metaphysical situation he abandons one of the basic ways in which humans become self-aware: by emotional and rational investment in language. The dreaminess of the poem, the gradual regression toward sleep, is the slope or angle of the speaker's declining sense of self. Renewal, perhaps, would be a function of sleep, but if so, it would only be a human sleep, not the more primal alternative of erasure evinced by the absent woodchuck.

It is no accident that the title of the poem following "After Apple-Picking" in *North of Boston* is "The Code." For Frost a code is always open to question, but he also recognizes its social and psychological utility. While "After Apple-Picking" deconstructs the code-relation between the symbol of desire and actual desire, "The Code" examines the semiology of social relations. The poems therefore complement each other—one by focusing on the psychological or metaphysical link between sign and psyche, the other by considering the social link between sign user and audience. However, unlike the "town-bred farmer" who is unaware of the code he has violated, the speaker of "After Apple-Picking" deliberately, out of respect for and acknowledgment of the rift between desire and the symbol of desire, rejects a code to which he has previously committed himself. By doing so, he opens himself to new possibilities, new poetics, but he also risks, in sleep, reconquest by the simple and perhaps necessary human mystification that makes language possible but condemns it to inadequacy.

Critics such as Marie Borroff have noted the prevalence of a more elaborate and Latinate vocabulary in Frost's later meditative poems, particularly in "Directive" (50). The presence of this vocabulary indicates a more analytical mode; the speaker of this complex poem more fully engages the reader by exposing his thought process as the basis of narration. The result is particularly intimate and dramatic, and the poem has earned much admiration. Randall Jarrell found it so compelling that he quoted it in its entirety in "To the Laodiceans" (46–48). And Frank Lentricchia argues that the poem makes a large thematic claim on the reader: "'Directive' is Frost's *summa,* his most compelling and encompassing meditation on the possibilities of redemption through the imagination, the one poem that a critic of Frost must sooner or later confront if he hopes to grasp the poet's commitment to his art as a way of saving himself, and to understand the astonishing unity of his life's work at last fully revealed here in this major poem of his later career" (112).

Lentricchia's powerful assertion is rhetorically almost as delicately constructed a performance as Frost's. By defining for "Directive" a powerful thematic and authorial hegemony, this statement becomes an extension of the poem, part of its history. The present essay will not attempt to controvert this claim, but merely will demonstrate an important facet of the poem's rhetorical strategies, its systematic rejection of the various claims of trope in order to gain the reader's confidence, and its embrace of a dialogic stance in which the speaker directs his attention simultaneously inward toward the meditative resources of the language and outward with the social resources of rhetoric.

The opening lines suggest how this doubleness will work, presenting backward and forward movements as one, as temporality and direction refuse to coincide:

> Back out of all this now too much for us,
> Back in a time made simple by the loss
> Of detail, burned, dissolved, and broken off
> Like graveyard marble sculpture in the weather,
> There is a house that is no more a house
> Upon a farm that is no more a farm
> And in a town that is no more a town. (1969, 377)

The ironic series of doublings, the "house that is no more a house," the "farm that is no more a farm," and the "town that is no more a town," is the designated predicate, while the combined attention of speaker and reader, the "us" of the first line, for whom together "all of this" is "now too much," in dialogic mutuality forms the subject.

Lines 8 through 40 explicate the narrative trope of the movement along the broken road to the ironic discovery of what the speaker already knows is there, the bogus Grail-goblet from which one might drink from the brook that is "cold as a spring as yet so near its source." Though the destination is entirely known to the speaker, this extended action of the dialogic subject demonstrates that the designated predicate, despite the repetition of doubling (line 45, for example: "Then for the house that is no more a house"), is anything but a fixed or known quality. For one thing, as in any version of the grail legend, the search for what Lentricchia calls "redemption through imagination" predominates over ostensibly religious motives, so that the speaker's attitude cannot be determined by the nature of the predicate but only by the verb movement toward revelation. The discovery of that attitude—an exposure of the speaker's psyche—is part of the process of modifying the predicate, not of the axiomatic though dialogic and therefore complex subject.

The subject, though, does divide and reunite at various points before it finds wholeness in the closure. It splits into traveler and guide in line 8 ("The road there, if you'll let a guide direct you") and suggests that the relationship between them is socially benign ("Who only has at heart your getting lost") rather than structurally disruptive. But "getting lost" is a step toward finding oneself and, further, a way of linking more indissolubly the two interlocutors, who will become "whole again beyond confusion" when they drink from the brook that is "Too lofty and original to rage." Finally cementing the relationship, fully enclosing the dialogue between speaker and addressee, is the purpose of this poem, and the journey over the broken road that "May seem as if it should have been a quarry" is a rhetorical one in that its main purpose is to impose the flow of dialogic narrative on the uneasy structures of tropes.

This dialogic narrative, established by the simple dramatic device of speaking to the reader as in an inclusive and confidential way, requires the supposition of a readerly memory similar to the speaker's—an understanding of the "all this" in the first line. It also requires confidence that the reader will share a faith in the ahistorical notion of a lost golden age in which the details of life (or death, like the details to "graveyard marble sculpture") were never fully and cumbersomely thrust upon the beholder. Surely these details are historical, but memory has fictionalized them. The utopian memory, which creates as well as recalls the golden age, thrives on this kind of fiction. This remaking through memory recalls the conventional invocation to the imagination that commonly frames myth, legend, and folk tale, an appeal for the imagination to displace worldliness. Yet the landscape of the subsequent journey is doggedly of this world, and the speaker's fanciful tropes (the personification of the "enormous Glacier," for instance) only serve to remind the reader that this poem is struggling to impose unreality on what is insistently actual.

The exposure of this struggle, and the obviously fanciful quality of the chosen tropes, weakens their force and makes it possible for the speaker to remind the reader not to take any of this too seriously ("You must not mind" and "Nor need you mind"). This suggests one of Frost's admonitions in "Education by Poetry" about the metaphor: "unless you are at home in the metaphor, unless you have had your proper poetical education in the metaphor, you are not safe anywhere" (1966, 39). The speaker of this poem has set about the task of educating the reader in the dangers of metaphor, which he will overcome for their mutual benefit. The threat of these tropes of presence, their coolness, the "ordeal" they present in their watchfulness, and their very occurrence in the poem challenge the rhetorically intimate relationship the early lines of the poem attempt to presume. The problem is to establish this intimacy of speaker and reader, despite the tendency of language to isolate and subjectify individual experience. In this regard, the Grail is the most challenging element in the poem, yet the one most subject to vanquishing by tone.

The establishment of a trope-defying tone is the key to the rhetorical success of the poem. Self-discovery, which in this poem requires the witness if not the actual connivance of the reader, will come only by defining the voice of the self as one that can confront and survive the various attempts at closure presented by successive heavily burdened tropes. The Grail is the most burdened, but before that the speaker and reader together have to run a gauntlet of absorptive, closure-inducing tropes. The Glacier, capitalized like a god, is a trope of time and other abstract dimensions; the cellar holes, which first as a group and then as a particular, more fully historicized instance, dominate the bulk of the poem, embody the failure of culture to maintain its temporary dominance over nature.

The forty cellar holes first encountered represent the continued peopling of this quasi-enchanted backland with ghosts. But their ghostliness is caught up and merged with the insistent life of the woods, so that the vague remnants of culture shade off into the heartier presence of nature. The speaker, by encouraging the reader and himself to "Make yourself up a cheering song of how / Someone's road home from work this once was," invites consideration of the domestic quality of actual human presence, which so entirely lacks the mystery suggested by the cellar holes as to separate them entirely from human significance. Thus the trope of lost culture, by its present mysterious indeterminacy, undermines its own historical link to that culture, undermines its very status as a trope.

The particular cellar hole, though, the goal-site of this journey, unfolds a more complex series of tropes of culture and human presence. The "children's house of make-believe" serves as a three-pronged metonymy of domesticity, imagination, and childhood, and provides a setting in which the dishes, "The playthings in the playhouse of the children," undermine the later appearance of the hidden drinking goblet, "like the Grail," by suggesting that artifacts, by their very survival in a place from which domesticity has fled, underscore the absence rather than assert the former historical presence of the human. The difference between the assertion of absence and the metonymy of former presence may seem merely one of rhetorical posture; but is significant with regard to the Grail-goblet, which for its privileged status as a religious artifact requires the ability to invoke not only human agency but the presence of the divine. The speaker, we learn, has stolen this goblet "from the children's playhouse," but the fact of its theft demonstrates that it is stealable and therefore still at least partly of the world of the domestic and of culture.

The description of the "belilaced cellar hole / Now slowly closing like a dent in dough" that once was a "house in earnest" suggests that the once inhabited, now abandoned site has lost its claim on human sympathy and begun to heal back into the world of nature. Its legitimacy or usefulness as a destination has passed, to be replaced with the brook, a product entirely and honestly of nature ("destination and . . . destiny"). The speaker, however, in presenting the loss of culture and its reversion into the alien world of nature toys with these brute categories in order to tease out the trope-shaped relationship between culture and destiny, both of which attempt to subvert nature. This playful indulgence assumes that the reader, who is also himself, understands that his destiny is separate from the failure of culture. This distinction between the social-cultural and the personal dimensions of this meditative poem requires a dialogic interplay of voices to impose a narrative discipline upon trope. But the speaker, assertive and intimate in the end, plays with the possibility that the concluding tropes—the cellar hole, the drinking goblet—would, if allowed their full degree of supplement, elegize and historicize the deaths of culture and religion, and thus leave the reader bereft of the world of culture. The reader would also remain separate from the speaker, since the central motif of elegy is the alienation of material and spiritual worlds, and the tropes of alienation necessarily acknowledge that state as one of special feeling.

The prescriptive admonition that closes the poem, however, admits the efficacy of narrative by completing the journey with a justifying act—the act of drinking—as if the whole purpose of this trip over rough country roads was to assuage a simple thirst. The actual purpose of the poem—to unite the dialogic voices of the poem, to link speaker and reader in a single entity—requires this confrontation with trope. The consequence of the play of metaphor is to assert the unifying power of narrative and force a closure independent of, yet informed by, an invoked array of cultural and religious possibilities.

Redemption through the imagination in "Directive" comes partly through the refusal to let trope dominate over the dialogic movement of the narrative. The meditative model for this poem is Wordsworth's secular idea of the imagination, and the integration of self—its disparities here represented by the functions of speaker and reader—requires the rhetorical dominance of this model over the trope-model of allegory and symbolism. By exploiting the poem's status as discourse and relying on the narrative interaction between speaker and reader, Frost avoids the limitations of trope-oriented models yet retains the power of trope to evoke larger worlds of discourse than those otherwise immediately available. By conflating the playful trope-awareness of poems like "After Apple-Picking" with a dialogic strategy, he retains the lyric evocation of privileged worlds of meaning without committing his poem to them, and yet avoids the narrowed because necessarily conversational rhetoric of the dramatic poem. Frost's inventiveness is nowhere greater, and, despite the desire of some critics to read him as a religious poet, nowhere does he make clearer the doggedly secular basis of his self-redemption.

"The Census-Taker"

Landscape in romantic and postromantic poetry generates characteristic rhetorical demands, most of which revolve about the trope of otherness represented by nature, the inscrutable Not-I. In many of Frost's best poems the spirit of place in New England has diminished to a landscape in which the capacity for human renewal apparently has faded, leaving the countryside littered with ruined farmhouses, dilapidated barns, and stone walls running through second-growth forest. Inhabiting this unpastoral scenery is a populace of brutal and unsuccessful farmers, their crazed and lonely wives, amateur witches, and eccentric telescopists. The region is scarred with hill farms abandoned when their owners died off or simply gave up trying to coax a profit from the recalcitrant and exhausted land. "The Census-Taker" is characteristic in its stance toward landscape, but it is archaeologically specific, and in the elegiac dignity of its blank verse it partially redeems a spiritually and humanly impoverished semiwilderness landscape through the historical sensitivity of the speaker and his morally attractive desire for "life to go on living." It is also, as Frank Lentricchia has pointed out, "as explicit a confrontation with nothingness as anything in modern American poetry" (1975, 80). Nothingness is the ultimate state of otherness, and confronting and besting it with the distinctly human project of language is one of the motives of Frost's poetry.

The relative wilderness of much of New England's hill country—its abandoned farmland and logging tracts, the mutability of the landscape and its shifting relationship to the idea of home—and the tendency of wilderness to suggest dispiriting and dehumanizing metaphors of the darker side of the human character occupy Frost from his earliest poems to the end of his career. No summary can convey the complexity of his exploration of these problems or the dignity—almost Miltonic, at times—of his elegant verse and the ingenuity with which it embodies and fulfills the poet's ambitious and skeptical vision.

But even a brief glance at some of Frost's other important wilderness poems illuminates the ambiguities of that vision and suggests why any reading of "The Census-Taker" is tentative at best. The "confrontation with nothingness," which usually in Frost's poetry stirs at least a response—usually an affirmative one—from the beholder, occurs in various forms. In "The Hill Wife" the nothingness is not that of an abandoned, cutover landscape but of madness, the nothingness of the mind confronted by its own sense of absence unmediated by otherness. For her, nature no longer represents otherness because her mind can no longer erect the barrier of her humanity between it and her. Essentially, she fails to keep metaphor in bounds and lets the landscape become sensate, even threateningly human, which in Frost's world dangerously exceeds the legitimate function of the imagination:

The tireless but ineffectual hands
 That with every futile pass
Made the great tree seem as a little bird
 Before the mystery of glass!

It had never been inside the room,
 And only one of the two
Was afraid in an oft-repeated dream
 Of what the tree might do. (1969, 128)

But this is Frost's most extreme reifying of the imagination, except perhaps for "The Witch of Coös." Most of his personae avoid this leap from metaphor to solipsism and instead confront nothingness as an external, decidedly nonhuman phenomenon.

In "Desert Places" a desolate field ("a few weeds and stubble") becomes "more lonely ere it will be less" as snow and night fall, giving this already desperate place "no expression, nothing to express" (1969, 296). Yet the speaker, like the traveler of "Stopping by Woods on a Snowy Evening," refuses the metaphor of landscape, a nothingness rigidly external to him. Although he is admittedly frightened by this bleakness, he recognizes that the source of his fear isn't emptiness as such, since the space "between stars" is truly empty and doesn't frighten him at all. Rather what frightens him is the unrealized possibility of habitation, the presence of a wasteland, a nothingness "so much nearer home"; while his presence at this site of nothingness and his sense of lost possibilities and role of purveyor of the idea of home make him experience the full force of this nothingness. The desert places he actually experiences are his "own," are functioning and undeniable metaphors of the possibility of internal absence—whether as madness, death, or merely detachment—within the self out of which he gazes into the falling night and falling snow. As Frost wrote to Louis Untermeyer in 1917, "I have neighed at night in the woods behind a house like vampires. But there are no vampires, there are no gnomes, there are no demons, there is nothing but me" (1964, 221).

In "The Wood-Pile," as previously noted, the speaker discovered a characteristic sign of human presence now become one of absence—a woodpile carefully measured and piled and propped and then apparently forgotten:

No runner tracks in this year's snow looped near it.
And it was older sure than this year's cutting,
Or even last year's or the year's before.
The wood was gray and the bark warping off it
And the pile somewhat sunken. Clematis
Had wound strings round and round it like a bundle.

But in this poem, unlike "The Census-Taker," the speaker rejects the role of spokesperson for the absent, refuses to lift his voice to those dreary and beautiful acres of swamp, refuses to accept that the wilderness, itself a stretch of dull gray, is graying this piled-up wood back to the torpor of the phenomenal world outside human experience and concerns. The speaker has already failed to incorporate into his own world the small bird, incompletely personified, flitting through the trees ahead of him, he has forgotten him for the comforting evidence of human endeavor, and now cannot easily let go of that comfort. Instead of accepting the likely death of the woodcutter, or at least the fact of failure to hold onto what was once won from the wilderness, he postulates an axeman "who lived in turning to fresh tasks," a person whose continued presence somewhere else we might take for granted; then, to make the best of his artifact's patent inutility, suggests that it might "warm the frozen swamp as best it could / With the slow smokeless burning of decay."

"The Census-Taker" is not only one of the bleakest but the most explicit of these wilderness confrontations. New England here has reverted to something like the "howling wilderness" encountered by early explorers and first settlers. Indeed, it is a New England in the process of reverting to, even reaffirming, that earlier condition. There is something satisfyingly pure about the encounter between humanity and the wilderness, and this purity wasn't lost on the Visible Saints of the Massachusetts Bay Colony. The census-taker is their secular descendant. His meditative voice doesn't dwell on religious matters but on humanist concerns, on the difficulty of maintaining a toehold of civilization in an abject waste.

The poem doesn't specify a particular place, but we might assume that it is a logging area somewhere in the far north of New England, probably in New Hampshire, since this poem is one of the "notes" to the longer poem of that title. Clearly the census-taker has walked a long way to get there; it is late in the day and presumably he will have to spend the night in this lonely place. The problem with which the poem climaxes, whether to "Break silence now or be forever silent" assumes a grim finality in this desolate place. Of course, the speaker breaks the silence by the very act of the poem but also by his expectation that life would "go on living," which eschews silence in favor of "The people that had loudly passed the door / [who] Were people to the ear but not the eye." This poem defines habitation not in the imagery of the eye but of sound. Many of the important indicators of presence or absence are verbs of sound—"whistle," "breathing," "said," "slammed," "rattled," "declare"— and the central question is whether to finally reject absence and "declare to the cliffs too far for echo" the speaker's self-endowed presence.

The poem opens on a windy evening on which the census-taker arrives at a crudely constructed, unfinished, and undersized house, isolated in a wasteland hacked out by loggers:

> I came an errand one cloud-blowing evening
> To a slab-built, black-paper-covered house
> Of one room and one window and one door,
> The only dwelling in a waste cut over
> A hundred square miles round it in the mountains:
> And that not dwelt in now by men or women.
> (It had never been dwelt in, though, by women,
> So what is this that I make a sorrow of?) (1969, 174)

The lack of past habitation by women indicts this tiny settlement for its indifference to the making of society and the reproduction of the human race. Despite the hacking and hewing done to the forest, this site does not represent the inroad of genuine civilization, only the preliminary masculine brutalizing of nature. This crude trope of culture is ineffective in itself because impermanent. Without the commitment to home, which requires the presence of both genders, conquest exhausts itself, leaving a silence and an open wound. Eventually, the land will reforest itself, healing the wound and refuting the human endeavor.

The census-taker, like the puritans disembarking in seventeenth-century New England, has a larger and more dignified purpose in his "errand into the wilderness." He has arrived not to pillage the forest for profit but to weigh the human against the natural element, to take the census, but is foiled by the failure of culture to survive the confrontation with nothingness:

> I came as census-taker to the waste
> To count the people in it and found none,
> None in the hundred miles, none in the house,
> Where I came last with some hope, but not much,
> After hours' overlooking from the cliffs
> An emptiness flayed to the very stone.

Unlike the puritans, however, the census-taker is not an apocalyptic. Frost's New England wilderness continually reasserts itself, reclaiming territory even if in somewhat mutilated condition. The diminishment is in grandeur and innocence: each reclamation is grimmer, more insistent, and even more inhospitable. The census-taker faces a wilderness of mutability not of entropy, and so is free to entertain the possibility of presence in the face of absence, a sense that what was once here could return, and indeed may linger in his very expectations. More immediate, though, in the early part of the poem is the desire to find the wilderness inhabited, to find a presence to offset the sheer absence, the disregard of humanity that characterizes nature. The problem, in part, is that nature itself is temporarily dysfunctional and cannot speak to him:

> The time was autumn, but how anyone
> Could tell the time of year when every tree
> That could have dropped a leaf was down itself
> And nothing but the stump of it was left
> Now bringing out its rings in sugar of pitch;
> And every tree up stood a rotting trunk
> Without a single leaf to spend on autumn,
> Or branch to whistle after what was spent.

This unnatural scene represents neither nature nor culture. The trees no longer process temporality, so the very seasons have lost their bearings, and the wilderness, in this unnatural state, refuses even the clearly delineated metaphorical role of otherness. This desolate, ambiguous state of being might illuminate the status of this abandoned house, but only because the previous human presence has mutilated the wilderness and has negated itself in doing so. The wind, an invisible but palpable presence that conventionally represents temporality and flux, narrates all the more effectively for the desolation:

> Perhaps the wind the more without the help
> Of breathing trees said something of the time
> Of year or day the way it swung a door
> Forever off the latch, as if rude men
> Passed in and slammed it shut each one behind him
> For the next one to open for himself.

As Lentricchia has argued in pairing this poem with "The Black Cottage," "the deserted house in both poems stimulates the creation of a house in the mind that will supply what the real thing can no longer supply: the sense of having locked out the dangerous world outside, the sense of being free from the cycles of process" (1975, 80). Process, in this instance, is the diminishment of spirit, and the spirit that fades finds its historical embodiment primarily in images of sound, which alone can overcome the most saddening quality of this wilderness, its unrelenting silence. The census-taker, in his agony of expectation, counts nine men in "dreamy unofficial counting": and finally a tenth, himself, then asks "Where was my supper? Where was anyone's?" and the momentary illusion fails.

It fails because the house is perfunctory—"one room and one window and one door"—and its contents suggest how truly perfunctory are the mere semiotics of habitation:

> No lamp was lit. Nothing was on the table.
> The stove was cold—the stove was off the chimney—
> And down by one side where it lacked a leg.

In his attempt to resist the full impact of the dreariness of the scene, the speaker acknowledges a deliberate if unconscious restriction of his senses so that he can avoid, for a while, admitting the hopelessness of his attempt to ward off a sinking sense of nothingness. "The people that had loudly passed the door" lack sufficient dimension to impress the eye, the prime organ of reality, and survive only in a collocation of negatives:

They were not on the table with their elbows.
They were not sleeping in the shelves of bunks.
I saw no men there and no bones of men there.

Exhausted by his attempt to account for absence, the speaker concedes that this uninhabited shell, with its museumlike, nonoperative appliances, is merely a token house, as if without its presence the land, though stripped of nature, would be lost even to the possibility of habitation. The census-taker has noted parenthetically that women never dwelt in this shell, so the possibility of procreation, of peopling this spot in some meaningful and self-sustaining way to compensate for the destruction of the trees, has never arisen. Cursed by the lack of human fecundity, the house stands as an ironic monument to its departed inhabitants. In crass economic terms the disappearance or nonappearance of the men who once lived there is readily explained by the exhaustion of the surrounding timber; yet absence has a mystery of its own, and it permeates everything the speaker beholds. It also constitutes a vital trope of his act of witness.

What dominates the poem, however, is not the lack of people but the innate dignity and humanizing voice of the speaker. He, the census-taker, is not merely a statistician: nor is he there only to consider the landscape with the "outward eye"; the eye, for example, of the naturalist who instead of mourning might rejoice at the absence of inhabitants (or would if the forest weren't depleted). Rather he is there to reexperience the act of habitation and affirm it as a peculiarly human act, one that momentarily separates us from the hundred square miles of wilderness just outside. The census-taker is like the person in Wallace Stevens's "Anecdote of the Jar" who "placed a jar in Tennessee / And round it was upon a hill," and found that it "took dominion everywhere." The house, like the jar, takes dominion through the speaker's sense of domesticity, which makes the temporarily inhabited place the center of his world.

The former inhabitants of this shabby frame house still exist as long as the census-taker can hold them in his mind, thought that isn't for long, since much as he inclines to the imagination of the ear he has to defer to the reality of the eye. These "people to the ear" have left signs not only of habitation but of absence as a palpable quality—the cold stove, the disconnected chimney, the lack of a lamp, the bare table, and the stub of an axe handle with which the speaker arms himself against ghosts—or against his own fear of absence. Insofar as this is a poem about absence it is inescapably about presence also, and the vague sense of the lingering spirit of habitation haunts the poem as surely as a ghost haunts its grave, so much so that the census-taker is moved to defend himself against a possibly hostile if physically minimal presence:

> I armed myself against such bones as might be
> With the pitch-blackened stub of an ax-handle
> I picked up off the straw-dust-covered floor.

Ironically, he arms himself against the ghost of that which he most desires, as if bones, harmless in themselves, might too cruelly insist on the failure of habitation to maintain its hold, the failure of "life to go on living." That this threat could assume a physical form is unlikely, but the power of metaphor here is almost overpowering, and the speaker acknowledges it.

Only the presence of the census-taker can bring both the actuality of absence and the possibility of presence into focus. Otherwise, the house-artifact lacks meaning; it is part of a sign-system that requires a reader to render it as a text. The story of ruins is a particularly hoary one, a familiar romantic motif, but here the empty house is not a synecdoche of a great empire; it is only a small, partly realized possibility, representing the melancholy of failure attending a pointless enterprise, the attempt to count souls where there are none. The question, as Poirier points out, is one of the "nature of a 'home' when there are almost no signs of life about it" (153). Here the signs of life are negative and minimal, though the census-taker has no trouble reading them. This house fails to define itself as a home because every sign points to absence and the failure to procreate. But as absence argues for its opposite, for presence, so the silence of uninhabitance demands the act of consciousness, the process of recognition that fills that silence with grief and a final, voiced desire. Every act is a determinedly human one, whether of self-defense, of holding the door shut, or of considering, of allowing himself to believe that something, after all, might be done to negate this onset of wilderness upon what was once an act of human defiance:

> Not bones, but the ill-fitted window rattled.
> The door was still because I held it shut
> While I thought about what to do that could be done—
> About the house—about the people not there.

This apparently desolate landscape, then, is a tabula rasa, a slate left blank by those who preceded the speaker and left him stranded like Gibbon amid the wreck of Rome and with a comparable responsibility to reaffirm, emotionally as well as historically, what once was:

> This house in one year fallen to decay
> Filled me with no less sorrow than the houses
> Fallen to ruin in ten thousand years
> Where Asia wedges Africa from Europe.

The speaker, like the protagonist of "The Most of It," has the opportunity to listen, as few ever do, to the sound of his own voice and see what he can make of it. And, like the protagonist of the later poem, the census-taker will find that reading signs requires an entirely human effort because it is preeminently a social act. Nature will give nothing except that which is so remote and inhuman that all one can say of it, as Frost says of the "great buck" that is the "embodiment" of something undetermined, is "that was all." Yet for the census-taker the sound of his own voice, though one of reconciliation rather than affirmation, is adequate to answer the wilderness, the absence, and the signs of past habitation:

> Nothing was left to do that I could see
> Unless to find that there was no one there
> And declare to the cliffs too far for echo,
> "The place is desert, and let whoso lurks
> In silence, if in this he is aggrieved,
> Break silence now or be forever silent.
> Let him say why it should not be declared so."

The cliffs that refuse to echo his cry, the hundred square miles of cutover waste, offer neither resistance to nor collaboration of his presence. The waste ground, the desert, ostensibly a sign of human penetration and the rationale for the existence of the house as well as an explanation of its abandonment, as anyone knows who has traversed the north country, is a landscape of the most painful and desolate absence because temporary human presence has devastated the landscape while withholding the consoling emotional plenitude of culture. The cliffs provide first a vantage point and later a monumentality that resists human reading. The text the speaker proposes is one in which nature occupies the present silence and in which human signs resist that silence in favor of a postulated or historical voice (the voice of the former inhabitants) and the present, and by default dominant, voice of the speaker. The poem reminds us that to speak, to postulate, to historicize, and to desire are human, while to maintain a monumental, unyielding silence is natural and therefore alien to us. And, inescapably, to propose a poem is to reject nature and landscape as distinct entities and attempt to resolve their silence by peopling places (personifying nature) that resist peopling.

Thoreau, on an errand comparable to the census-taker's, found the Maine wilderness more resistant than he had expected, more resolutely nonhuman than he had imagined:

> It was a relief to get back to our smooth, but still varied landscape. For a permanent residence, it seemed to me that there could be no comparison between this and the wilderness, necessary as the latter is for a resource and a background, the raw material of all our civilization. The wilderness is simple, almost to barrenness. The partially cultivated country it is which chiefly has inspired, and will continue to inspire, the strains of poets, such as compose the mass of any literature. . . . A civilized man . . . with his ideas and associations, must at length pine there, like a cultivated plant, which clasps its fibers about a crude and undissolved mass of peat. (134)

Frost, when he's not apocalyptic (as in "Fire and Ice"), is almost consistently Thoreauvian; but in this poem, I must repeat, civilization is not the fact of pastoral inhabitation but the fact of consciousness. The speaker's insistence on humanist values distinguishes him from the landscape he temporarily inhabits, enables him to read and understand the signs of a limited mode of domesticity, and leads him to confront the crux of meditation, the possibility of exerting his voice not to intimidate the wilderness (it can't be intimidated) but to express once again the human resistance to silence, against noncommunion and suspicion of the rhetorical urgency embodied as and represented by the poem itself. Even the speaker's "melancholy of having to count souls / Where they grow fewer and fewer every year" is affirmative, but that the melancholy should be "extreme where they [the souls] shrink to none at all" triggers the census-taker's declaration that "It must be I want life to go on living."

Frost is no Wordsworth: his epiphanies occur not to illuminate the spirit that moves all things but to spite nature, to fling humanist values in the face of that human indifference. Wordsworth well understood how separately the human imagination stands from nature, but whereas he read nature as the census-taker reads the relics in the cottage, Frost insists almost to a Blakean degree on the imagination as the originating force and the inhabiting voice as the primary source of knowledge and insight. The protagonist of "The Most of It" begins by understanding that "He . . . kept the universe alone," and if he had fully recognized the truth of that he would not have expected to raise a voice in nature in reply. Unlike the census-taker, he receives an echo, but the sign, the embodiment that is the swimming buck, has nothing to say to him. Its attributes are those that are proper to it, but they are the attributes of the nonhuman world— bestial power, monumentality, and a certain unrelenting purpose. No "counterlove" need be expected, and this is Frost's reply to Wordsworth, who in the *Prelude,* though overshadowed by grave, indifferent forms, experiences a form of communion Frost cannot entertain:

> And as I rose upon the stroke my boat
> Went heaving through the water like a swan—
> When from behind that craggy steep, till then
> The bound of the horizon, a huge cliff,
> As if with voluntary power instinct,
> Upreared its head. I struck, and struck again,
> And growing still in stature, the huge cliff
> Rose up between me and the stars, and still
> With measured motion, like a living thing
> Strode after me. (1805, Book 1)

Frost would not allow a cliff to stride after him like a living thing. To succumb to this illusion would suggest he had fallen prey to madness, like the lonely hill wife. But even indifference is a personifying quality, since nature reflects every attitude we bring to it, and the wilderness in "The Census-Taker" is partly the product of the human effort of logging, and the census-taker in his meditation cannot help but partially reclaim that wasteland for civilization. In meditation and the rhetoric of its expression, a rhetoric shaped by confrontation with the wilderness, lies his power over what he sees. The spirit of New England is the human consciousness contemplating the howling wilderness, whether inhabited by the devil, by hostile or at least unchristian Indians, or simply by an imperturbable silence.

The speaker of "The Census-Taker" is distinct from what he beholds, and in that distinction lies his humanity. He wields his rhetoric like a lucky charm, and postulates that whoever is hidden in this wilderness— whether the ghosts or the corporeal bodies of past inhabitants or himself, most especially—might speak and declare that this place should *not* be declared a desert, should instead be accounted an inhabited place, or at least a place of presence. In the extremity of his grief, his melancholy at finding no "souls" to count (much as a puritan minister might have become melancholic for lack of converted saints to listen to him preach), the census-taker declares himself quintessentially human and forever peoples this place by declaring that here, in this otherwise uninhabited wasteland, he has understood that he wants "life" against all clear signs of abandonment "to go on living." Like the speakers of many of Frost's other important poems, the census-taker understands that human presence requires certain rhetorical strategies to define itself, and that in the absence of a challenging voice to acknowledge the signs of culture— abandoned houses, an abandoned woodpile, a lone drinking cup—exterior and interior wilderness will dominate the silence.

Stevens

Allegorical Landscape and Myth

As Wallace Stevens's poem "Phosphor Reading by His Own Light" notes, "It is difficult to read. The page is dark. / Yet he knows what it is that he expects." The page, the otherness that is the perceptual world, is difficult to interpret. The reader "knows" what is there, brings certain expectations to the page; but how can Phosphor, a creature of imagination and self-illumination, distinguish his own desires, internally reflecting his own light, from the external world brightened by his imagination? This a crucial issue because, as Stevens says in "The Noble Rider and the Sound of Words," "The imagination loses vitality as it ceases to adhere to what is real" (1951, 6).

The imagination is a troublesome processor of information, yet an essential light source that sparks everything vital and human in us. It not only illuminates the dark of the exterior world but resists the grimness of nature and its antipathy to culture. Without "the imagination pressing back against the pressure of reality" culture and civilization would collapse in violence (36). Stevens spent his distinguished career as Phosphor reading that dark page with a critical sense of the relationship between external and internal worlds, and a conviction that in "the sound of words" lies human salvation. Rather than trying to fix that relationship in a syllogism, his poems explore it through the reinvention—in terms particularly suitable to American culture and landscape—of a rhetoric of allegory and myth independent and critical of European and Christian traditions.

This chapter focuses on two instances of Stevens's ambitious and complex program, his empowerment of the most ordinary landscapes through allegory, and his attempt in *Notes Toward a Supreme Fiction* to demonstrate that the imperative of the creation myth is one of the basic forces of imagination. I hope also to suggest how Stevens, in placing his speakers in landscapes of particular texture and dimension, devises rhetorical strategies that link the speaking self (the subject) with landscape (the object) in terms that, rather than pictorializing or psychologizing, mediate between those categories to generate a fictional entity, a mythlike structure that embodies one important aspect of that grand "supreme fiction" to which Stevens devoted his poetic life.

Connecticut in Stevens's Poetry

"Spring in Connecticut is just as wild as spring in Persia," Wallace Stevens once wrote in a fit of exuberance (1966, 679). Though disappointed that the spring of 1950 wasn't·as bright as he had hoped it would be, he still felt moved to invoke his love of the exotic on behalf of his adopted state. Milton Bates, however, in considering the role of the Connecticut landscape in Stevens's poetry, argues that, despite the affection revealed in the late radio script "Connecticut Composed," Stevens "Deep down . . . belonged to the wood and stone of Pennsylvania rather than Connecticut" (288). While Stevens's lingering affection for the Pennsylvania of his childhood is undeniable, Bates here confounds a somewhat sentimental love of actual scenery with the reinvention of landscape and renewal of self in the larger terms of Stevens's aesthetic. Poets of place, with whom Stevens accurately identified himself, tend to bond quickly and deeply to their immediate locales because the contemplating mind engenders the poem by reshaping with gusto the particular qualities of available land forms.

Connecticut offers an unspectacular landscape. In "Connecticut Composed," Stevens, describing a train ride across the state, finds the landscape to be minimalist, punctuated most prominently by the acts of culture, not of nature:

> Everything seemed gray, bleached and derelict and
> the word *derelict* kept repeating itself as part of the
> activity of the train. But this was a precious ride
> through the character of the state. The soil every-
> where seemed thin and difficult and every cutting
> and open pit disclosed gravel and rocks, in which

> only the young pine trees seemed to do well. There
> were chicken farms, some of them abandoned, and
> there were cow barns. The great barns of other
> states do not exist. There were orchards of apples
> and peaches. Yet in this sparse landscape with its
> old houses of gray and white there were other
> houses, smaller, fresher, more fastidious. (1989, 303)

The fastidious little houses thrive in this unadorned landscape, much as
Stevens's imagination does. Plain, unsentimental, provincial, or colorless
landscapes suffice for the mythmaking poet as well as, perhaps better than,
settings idealized by history, ancestral piety, or unusual physical beauty.
This is one reason why Stevens's poems of Connecticut attain a mythic
aura more powerful than that of Robert Lowell's early poems about Boston, for example, and resistant to the totalizing aesthetic of realism found
in Williams's poetry of industrial New Jersey and Hart Crane's urbanized
epic meditations on the myth of American cultural hegemony.

Geographical tropes, for romantic-modernist poets, tend to fuse
the immediate with the elusive or the ineffable. The Hartford that Robert Lowell described, in reference to Stevens, as "like Boston, only worse,
and more parochialized, by the insurance companies themselves" (1987,
209), was not the Hartford of the imagination. The latter, like New Haven and the "River of Rivers in Connecticut," is a fusion, under pressure,
to make what Stevens refers to in "Someone Puts a Pineapple Together"
as "the total artifice [that] reveals itself / As the total reality."

Stevens's philosophical bent often leads him to imitate a metaphysical argument that has usually been taken to be the subject, and, until
Helen Vendler in *Wallace Stevens: Words Chosen Out of Desire* clearly defined the passion of his language, seemed to preclude emotion as a central
issue in his most important work. However, the placement of the meditative self in the landscape not only constitutes the mise-en-scène of the
poems, especially after *Harmonium,* but the basic situation of metaphor,
in which the imagination and reality most fully engage each other.

The trope of geography is not one of description but of action. The
specific nature of a setting determines, to a great extent, the action possible within it, the undulation of the resultant meditation. For this purpose, Connecticut served as well as Pennsylvania, or perhaps better, since

Stevens seems to find it a malleable backdrop, a place that resists too great a pressure of reality (as New York City might), yet exerts a sufficient degree of the commonplace. In certain key poems, especially in the last two collections, Stevens's adopted state became central to the conception and execution because of the particular nature of the landscape and the lack (for him) of immediate pressing historical, social, and cultural implications.

It is safe to say that these poems would have been at least slightly different if Stevens's central meditative voice had found itself in another setting. "The River of Rivers in Connecticut," "An Ordinary Evening in New Haven," and "Of Hartford in a Purple Light" derive certain of their qualities from the particularity, different in each instance, with which Stevens embraces the Connecticut setting. He does not resort to description in the manner of Wordsworth or even of William Carlos Williams, upon one of whose themes he once wrote "nuances." Connecticut, in each of these poems, is not a site of picturesque scenery or finely distinguished details but a "region full of intonings," a place without description but full of mysterious light, a place in which desire, imagination, and the world come together in ways that in the later stages of Stevens's career seem increasingly certain yet immensely complex, generating scenes of innumerable shadings.

"Of Hartford in a Purple Light" vaguely hints at a response to Archibald MacLeish's "You, Andrew Marvell," and illustrates the great compression often found in Stevens's shorter poems of the 1930s. It is a poem about learning to see landscape, and about seeing as an act of creation that occurs in the light of the revealed world. The speaker, who humbles himself by addressing the sun as "Master" (always an ironic title in Stevens's work), assumes the role of the poet who interprets the light in terms of his own perceptions, which mingle quotidian actuality (town, river, railroad) with operatic coloration and the frank artifice of personification:

> A long time you have been making the trip
> From Havre to Hartford, Master Soleil,
> Bringing the lights of Norway and all that.
>
> A long time the ocean has come with you,

Shaking the water off, like a poodle,
That splatters incessant thousands of drops,

Each drop a petty tricolor. For this,
The aunts in Pasadena, remembering,
Abhor the plaster of the western horses,

Souvenirs of museums. But, Master, there are
Lights masculine and lights feminine.
What is this purple, this parasol,

This stage-light of the Opera?
It is like a region full of intonings.
It is Hartford seen in a purple light.

A moment ago, light masculine,
Working, with big hands, on the town,
Arranged its heroic attitudes.

But now as in an amour of women
Purple sets purple round. Look, Master,
See the river, the railroad, the cathedral . . .

When male light fell on the naked back
Of the town, the river, the railroad were clear.
Now, every muscle slops away.

Hi! Whisk it, poodle, flick the spray
Of the ocean, ever-freshening,
On the irised hunks, the stone bouquet. (1954, 226)

Understanding this poem requires accepting the preposterous manner with which it imitates a Dickensian servant's slyly humble address to his master. This address concludes with an imitation of the voice in which one might "Hi!" away an even lowlier servant to do the master's bidding, in this instance the poet "Hi"-ing away the ocean. The difficulty of taking seriously this kind of rhetorical play may be why this poem has rarely been discussed by Stevens critics. But almost alone among Stevens's poems of this period it manifests an aspect of the poet's relationship with reality that will become more apparent in *Notes Toward a Supreme Fiction*. The poet, Stevens emphasizes, is the servant of reality, and imagination, which the earlier romantics elevated to so noble a role, is for Stevens simply the means by which the poet maintains composure in the face of the bright light, the enormous pressure, of the real. The imagination functions as a sense of humor might function to keep a servant from despair. By mediating between reality and desire, the imagination makes poetry possible, but it also prevents the light of the sun from simplifying or occluding reality.

The servant, not the master, understands the dichotomy of "Lights masculine and lights feminine," and understands that the purple that envelopes Hartford is the light of the sun translated (as through a prism) by his imagination to represent his desire for the feminine, while the "heroic attitudes" embody his vision of the masculine. The relationship between masculine power and feminine complexities of coloration are problematic, but probably not as insistently Freudian as some critics have claimed. The masculine-feminine dichotomy is a product of culture, not of nature, and is a fiction, unlike the sun. Could his imagination have illuminated New York in similar shades of purple? Perhaps only a "town," not a city, readily accepts being arranged into "heroic attitudes." It is not difficult to believe that the pressure of reality exerted by New York, because already shaped into attitudes larger than the merely heroic, would resist such embellishment. Hartford, in this instance, is a suitable site of contention between the will of the sun, which resists the differentiations of culture, and the desire of the poet, which imaginatively distinguishes things, colors, and forms of rhetoric. That he also seems to fear the feminine as a diminution of the masculine underscores the courage necessary to acknowledge this distinction, which the harsh light of the sun would otherwise obliterate. Generating the supreme fiction requires that desire and reality negotiate on roughly equal terms.

The title of "The River of Rivers in Connecticut," as Ronald Sukenick aptly notes, indicates that its subject "flows through Connecticut, as well as everywhere else" (196). Yet it is a river that if mythic in one dimension is decidedly geographical in another, and occupies space as well as mind, though in a locale that is not entirely natural, where there are "trees that lack the intelligence of trees." The trees, as Stevens suggested in a commentary, grow in an unnatural place, and therefore lack that bond with nature that allows them to share in its vast, somewhat undifferentiated, intelligence. That is because here above the first black cataracts nature is beginning to yield to culture, and reality and the imagination begin to interact. The tone of the poem is that of the geography lesson, which suggests we accept a certain yielding to the pressure of reality; but the necessity of reminding the reader that this river is not the Styx (but rather is a river on the near side, reality's side, of Stygia) suggests how porous is the membrane between the mythic and the real, and how inexact is Stevens's aphorism that "Reality is a cliché / From which we escape by metaphor" (1989, 204).

Sukenick argues that the metaphorically vital river represents the flow of "existence," and that it "consists of the tangible reality of common objects, such as 'The Steeple at Farmington,' and the town of Haddam" (196). However, in my reading of the poem the river does not represent existence (or, as Vendler puts it, "the total stream of life" [1984, 74]) but rather is the force in landscape that mediates between geographical actuality and the desire for landscapes of the imagination. Metaphor is no longer about the relationship between tenor and vehicle, that neat but obfuscating binary complement. Another late poem dismisses that binary relationship by defining metaphor "Not [as] Ideas About the Thing but the Thing Itself," a "scrawny cry from outside" that invites the imagination to claim it as its own.

The action of "The River of Rivers in Connecticut" (1954, 533) is nothing less than the rediscovery of much of Connecticut (a state both of desire and of reality) through the process of mediating between landscape and desire. Mock pedantry gives way to an argument about the way landscape and the imagination interact, which then concludes with a marriage of elements—light and air—and a moment of transcendence. Faced with particulars—the steeple at Farmington (which incidentally is not on the Connecticut River but on its own tributary) and the village of Haddam—the imagination interacts with the river, the emblem of vital natural and cultural (mythic) force, and of these two vitalities engenders a "third commonness with light and air, / A curriculum," a plan, a program, "a vigor, a local abstraction." The state of Connecticut, a political and cultural abstraction represented by two actual place names, is regenerated by the river that flows everywhere and nowhere, that never exhausts itself but does change its shape.

I do not agree with Harold Bloom that this poem "accepts the myth of Stygia, region of the river Styx, in order to transcend the role of Charon and the oblivion of Hades" (1977, 365). Rather, the poem reminds us of the myth only to refute it and assert that "there is no ferryman," and "No shadows walk on its banks"; the myth is unoccupied, therefore defunct, and the river-as-process is not bound to the past. Bloom aptly describes the river as a "trope of power," but it is particularly a figure of the combined power of geographical actuality and the imagination. The myth of Stygia was the product of that combination once, long ago, but the new myth is Connecticut, that "local abstraction" generated by light and air.

If, as Bloom contends, this Connecticut is a "transcendence," what is transcended are the relative limitations of geography and the imagination. The geography lesson concludes, then, with the irony that the curriculum linking reality and the imagination transforms the river into a sea—a wry comment, perhaps, on the "oceanic feeling" Bloom quotes from Freud. Wry because this transformation negates the original metaphoric value of the river and redirects its power—or rather negates its power by forcing it to relinquish its form. Perhaps this is why myths like that of Stygia grow stale—it is the making of myth, the curriculum, the confrontation of imagination with the glistening of the steeple, the shining of the village, that engenders the naming that in turn stalls the river, broadens it into sealike stasis. Transcendence balances reality and the imagination to generate an entity that is neither, but that abstract state is momentary, at best, and its price is the depletion of the vitality of its originating metaphor.

Connecticut, then, attains the status of myth, as Stygia long ago did, but this new visionary quality is a product of light and air, and is not a permanent state. As Stevens says in "Connecticut Composed," "We live in the tradition which is the true mythology of the region and we breathe in with every breath the joy of having ourselves been created by what has been endured and mastered in the past" (1989, 303). Myth, which is constantly being re-created by the pressure of desire, represents the past and links it to the present, but it is a living process, begat by and begetting living beings. Because it is culture not nature, myth cannot sustain trees, and because the fatefulness of the river is that it flows from myth (culture) to reality (nature) and back again, trees cannot thrive on its banks. But the river's "propelling force" is the pressure of reality not of myth, and only that moment of closure, when the pressure of poetry and the imagination is greatest (a recurring structural principle in Stevens's late lyrics), can stall it "like a sea."

The New Haven of "An Ordinary Evening in New Haven" (1954, 465) is twofold: it is "The eye's plain version . . . the vulgate of experience," the reality of a shabby industrial city between Hartford and New York; it is a place where we might "Suppose these houses are composed of ourselves, /So that they become an impalpable town," a place (or state) of imaginative redemption. The bulk of the poem mediates between these two New Havens. Because it is an ordinary evening, this mediation, we may assume, is part of ordinary experience; in fact, as the poem progresses, it seems to be the necessary state of existence. Helen Vendler argues that the poem is concerned with aging and depletion, and that the poem sets itself the difficult task of "accounting, in terms of consciousness, for a depression which is overwhelmingly physical—the metabolic depletion in age of the body's responses" (1969, 271). Because the scenery itself is so depleted, because "These Houses, these difficult objects, dilapidate / Appearances of what appearances," they link themselves metaphorically to the poet, who is a house composed of the sun and yet a house like these other houses, collapsing under the pressure of reality.

The flux of metaphor, then, mingles the dominant tropes—those of the dark, the body as dilapidated house, and light, the house made of sun. New Haven, though a physical town, boasts "metaphysical streets." But neither the physical nor the metaphysical vision alone suffices to account for the depletion, the "barrenness" that "is an exposing," "a coming on and a coming forth." Depletion, a human entropy, would hardly return as "a clearness" that "stands restored" (section XXX). Imagination is a state of grace not a fixed dimension, but it is the human half of the world, a place of elemental desire. We keep "coming back to the real" because its clarity corrects the blinding sunlit narcissism of desire, but reality does not monopolize the world—it is not simply a matter of the mind versus the planet. While the poem does not quite commit itself, it raises the possibility that "reality exists / In the mind," and that "Real and unreal are two in one" (section XXVIII). Yet even if reality exists in the mind it does not wholly constitute it, nor does the mind entirely constitute the world. The poem notes that "The sun is half the world," and "New Haven is half sun," though the other half, the dark half, is slightly more real because "lighted by space" rather than by the sun, which complies with the imagination. The mind describes, even inscribes a place (as on a post-card), but does not embody it.

As the poem progresses, the imagery of light and dark, dilapidation and sun, find embodiments distant from physical New Haven, as the "land of the lemon trees" (sun imagery), for example, or the "squirrels, in tree-caves" that "Huddle together in the knowledge of squirrels" (that is, who brood in dark dilapidated houses). Eventually, the poem (in section XXXI) concludes by arguing that subtleties of perception and art approach the final form of reality by reconceiving and revising it, finding form without fixation, perhaps as a tone or coloring. The resolution to the state of depression, languor, and self-depletion is to demonstrate that the two New Havens complement and inhere in each other—to deconstruct the metaphor of the self as a dilapidated house, deconstruct as well the self as house composed of sun, and demonstrate how these are in fact the same house. The labyrinthine argument is too extended and complex to summarize here, but for purposes of this essay it is useful to consider the forms in which the qualities of New Haven and its setting (especially its night sky), both the New Haven of dilapidated houses and the one that like the poet's imagination is made of sun, recur.

Sections I and II present the two New Havens and summarize the difficulties of telling them apart:

> Obscure, in colors whether of the sun
> Or mind, uncertain in the clearest bells,
> The spirit's speeches, the indefinite,
>
> Confused illuminations and sonorities,
> So much ourselves, we cannot tell apart
> The idea and the bearer-being of the idea.

New Haven is half light, half dark, both idea and the bearer of the idea. As such, it would seem to be the perfect embodiment of the balance between reality and imagination that ignites the moment of transcendence in "The River of Rivers in Connecticut," but it is also a city of particular qualities that in some ways obfuscate, in some ways promote the desire that leads to effective confrontation with the real. Section IV argues, roughly, that people living in places like New Haven have trouble shaping their desire, although the very voice of desire is satisfying because it calls attention to otherness:

> Plain men in plain towns
> Are not precise about the appeasement they need.
>
> They only know a savage assuagement cries
> With a savage voice; and in that cry they hear
> Themselves transposed, muted and comforted
>
> In a savage and subtle and simple harmony,
> A matching and mating of surprised accords,
> A responding to a diviner opposite.

For Stevens "savage" means closer to the idea (not the fact) of origin, and it is apt that a savage voice should transpose, mute, and comfort, and give rise to a "savage and subtle and simple harmony," the very sort of harmony he seeks to generate in these late poems. Certainly, the anaphora points to Stevens's central lifelong concern with finding a language adequate for expressing that which precedes and follows language: the recurrent idea of origin, the depletion of the imagination under the pressure of reality.

The people of New Haven, "plain men" in a plain town, confront the world without (for example, the projection of tropical luxuriance, which has to be imagined later in the poem), but they do have architecture and culture, Yale and everything it represents. Section VII offers the city's cultural institutions as sources of interpretation of the "Naked Alpha" with which the experience of reality begins, as well as the "hierophant Omega" where it concludes:

> In the presence of such chapels and such schools,
> The impoverished architects appear to be
> Much richer, more fecund, sportive and alive.

But these cultural monuments are not the only forms after which we model our experience. In fact, they and other external manifestations of form reinforce a rather commonplace notion of reality:

The objects tingle and the spectator moves
With the objects. But the spectator also moves
With lesser things, with things exteriorized

Out of rigid realists. It is as if
Men turning into things, as comedy,
Stood, dressed in antic symbols, to display

The truth about themselves, having lost, as things,
That power to conceal they had as men,
Not merely as to depth but as to height

As well, not merely as to the commonplace
But, also, as to their miraculous,
Conceptions of new mornings of new worlds.

New Haven tempts us to "fling ourselves, constantly longing, on this form," on commonplace reality. The streets breathe it, and we breathe the breath of the streets, so "We keep coming back and coming back / To the real: to the hotel instead of the hymns / That fall upon it out of the wind." Tempted by powerfully concrete manifestations, we "seek the poem of pure reality, untouched / By trope or deviation" and attempt to link word and object in a simple but impossible bond.

But like seekers of real toads in imaginary gardens we can enter the metaphysical streets of physical New Haven, and through the imagination see real things more fully, more as themselves. "Juda becomes New Haven, or else must" because the "profoundest forms" are the product of metaphysical seeing. Only a town that could remind one of Juda and yet still be made of the most commonplace reality could satisfy Professor Eucalyptus, who looks for god in a shabby room in New Haven, whose pantheism suggests the aesthetic that rejects trope and would embrace the word as if embracing the thing itself:

The dry eucalyptus seeks god in the rainy cloud.
Professor Eucalyptus of New Haven seeks him
In New Haven with an eye that does not look

Beyond the object. He sits in his room, beside
The window, close to the ramshackle spout in which
The rain falls with a ramshackle sound. He seeks

God in the object itself, without much choice.
It is a choice of the commodious adjective
For what he sees, it comes in the end to that.

Clearly, New Haven lends itself to this sort of seeking because it is
so utterly, temptingly commonplace, a "dilapidation of dilapidations." This
is precisely the city Stevens requires for his musing on self-dilapidation
and the temptation to allow the imagination to wither under the pressure
of reality. Its very ordinariness tempts the ephebe to envision something
beyond it. Just as the free verse of "An Ordinary Evening in New Haven" slyly suggests blank verse to the eye and ear but refuses its formal
confinement, so the city itself suggests larger ideas of form, larger ideas of
reality than it actually embodies. The pressure of reality is not as great
here as it first appears, just as the poem's verse is not so restrictive as it
appears. If one brings "a strong mind" to "a weak neighborhood," one is
able to define "a fresh spiritual" and distinguish "The actual landscape
with its actual horns" and get "at an essential integrity." Because "Real
and unreal are two in one: New Haven / Before and after one arrives,"
because places are utterly implicated by our perceptions of them, it is
difficult to sort out their reality from our continual processing of that
reality, "This endlessly elaborating poem" that "Displays the theory of
poetry, / As the life of poetry." Theory and life are not quite the same
(though in an aphorism in "Adagia" Stevens asserts that "The theory of
poetry is the theory of life" [1989, 202]), and yet a "More harassing
master" can demonstrate that they are the same, that the process of linking the imagination and reality through the mind generates tropical worlds
of luxuriance in which the theory of poetry is the theory of life. New
Haven, however, is itself a severe master, and the poem keeps returning to
it, edging and inching toward "final form," which will be a version of
New Haven in which form is not a fixation but a tone or coloring, "a
force that traverses a shade."

If the actual New Haven hadn't existed, some other shabby industrial town with a college would have done as well, perhaps. But New Haven is paradigmatic. It manifests the most commonplace reality and yet contains numerous distinguished versions of Professor Eucalyptus musing upon the ineffable. Stevens knew the city mostly from passing through it on the train from Hartford to New York. Because the train always stopped for a fairly lengthy period to change engines (from steam to electric) before the trip under Park Avenue to Grand Central, and again on the way back, Stevens must often have sat staring out at the dirty, brown brick station, the big, plain hotel on the west side of the green, and the Harkness Tower a few blocks beyond.

In progressing from a commonplace, brick-textured foreground to the hotel of reality to the reaching for the ineffable represented by Yale's neo-Gothic architecture, this view embodies the movement the poem works out, more or less, in its complex meditative drama. The perspective of the poem, then, derives from an actual situation, and imitates in its rhetoric the contemplating mind that is merely passing through on the way somewhere else, for which New Haven is "a sense in the changing sense / Of things." Before reaching New Haven, a sense of its reality forms in the imagination. There, for a brief period, the utterly mundane scene overwhelms the imagination. Then, after the train has moved on toward New York or Hartford, the New Haven of the imagination returns in revitalized form. A lifetime's worth of trips to New York generated the complexities of this meditation, train trips Stevens described in terms conducive to self-renewal: "I went to New York last week. Only to sit on the train and look out of the window gets one over these occasional periods of restlessness" (1966, 692).

For Stevens, then, Connecticut consisted of light and dark, a state of the real and a state of the imagination. No distinction between these is other than momentary, fluid, "imaginary poles," oppositions that last only as long as the perception of them. Transcendence, which renders the landscape and the mind as a single entity, and which maps metaphysical streets over real ones, is a difficult state to engender and impossible to maintain for long. Stevens, though a poet of place, does not commit himself to living in the hotel of reality; but when he requires the particulars of a place to manifest themselves he finds that the "gray bleached derelict" qualities of his adopted state are sometimes those that best serve him. More significantly, he seems to find an aesthetic parallel in the Connecticut landscape to the plainness of voice that in the period of "The Rock" suits him better than the gaudier rhetoric of *Harmonium* or even "Of Hartford in a Purple Light." The plainest landscapes, human or natural, display the subtlest gradations of tone and coloring. Because Stevens argues that "a mythology reflects its region," it is safe to assume that the mythmaking of his late poetry that grows out of his confrontation with real and imagined Connecticut assumes a form peculiar to that relationship. "A Mythology Reflects Its Region," the penultimate poem of *The Palm at the End of the Mind,* argues that the creator of the myth is himself created by the landscapes, actual or imagined, in which he renews himself, as Stevens renews himself in dilapidated New Haven, and becomes the landscape as the landscape becomes an extension of him:

> A mythology reflects its region. Here
> In Connecticut, we never lived in a time
> When mythology was possible—But if we had—
> That raises the question of the image's truth.
> The image must be of the nature of its creator.
> It is the nature of its creator increased,
> Heightened. It is he, anew, in a freshened youth
> And it is he in the substance of his region,
> Wood of his forests and stone out of his fields
> Or from under his mountains. (1984, 398)

To be a creator, though not the Creator, is to live again in a "freshened youth," to be one with fields and mountains, to become the "substance of his region." Because the landscape is neither more nor less than its image, because the real is not the commonplace but a bond between desire and perception, because Connecticut is a region not only of wood and stone (surely indistinguishable from the wood and stone of Pennsylvania mentioned by Bates) but of humanly formed images, it is an adequate force field in which to generate a mythology. The coy disclaimer that "we never lived in a time / When mythology was possible" readily yields to "But if we had" and to the larger argument that humanity is a mythmaking species that is perpetually renewing its mythology by increasing and heightening itself and its vision of its surroundings, as Stevens heightens the commonplace Connecticut of derelict landscape into a landscape of purple light. As the elegant "Dutch Graves in Bucks County" makes clear, Stevens did not allow Connecticut to replace Pennsylvania in his affections; but his affections for places were varied and complex, and his aesthetic was large enough to make room for—and good use of—his adopted state.

Notes Toward a Supreme Fiction

As Marianne Moore points out in her perceptive 1942 review of the Cummington edition of Notes Toward a Supreme Fiction, in Stevens's work "imagination and the imaginer are different from images and imagers" (380). The process of imagining, rather than the realized images, shapes and dominates the poem. Because her review concerns itself primarily with the efficacies of Stevens's visual and aural imagery, and justly praises Stevens for finding the language to match his powerful imaginer's eye, "the center of a circle spread / To the final full," Moore does not attempt to account for the larger circle, the narrative inscribed by the poem, though her comments on his concern with heroes and heroism suggest awareness of his greater purpose.

In recent years critics such as Helen Vendler, Milton Bates, and Barbara Fisher have called attention to Stevens's passionate language and the underlying emotional imperative of his poetry. The passion with which Stevens formulates his imagery inheres, for example, in Notes in his rejection of the "face of slate," the "lasting visage in a lasting bush," and the "face of stone" that seem to embody the frozen gaze, the imaginer too enthralled by the image he either projects or perceives (1954, 400). This face is the victim of an eye that "could not escape, a red renown," a sensibility too refined, perhaps, or too narcissistic, too obsessed with its own elegant function, perhaps even too humanist in its regard of the universe.

The generating force behind this passion is the narrative, allegorical movement of the poem, which critics in Stevens's lifetime did not describe, and which few critics since have explicitly addressed—most treating the poem as a sequence of discrete and sometimes incomplete poems rather than as the single movement Stevens did not exactly intend but nonetheless orchestrated. The narrative, which imitates the temporal flow of meditation, represents the presence of the poet. Without it, the poem would be a series of ruminations lacking the larger commitment that makes the passion of Stevens's rejection of imaginative stasis palpable. These ruminations, as they stand, often seem individually inconclusive, since they are committed to the larger structure of the poem rather than to lyric closure. So ambitious a poem must in some way represent the whole poet because, as Stevens argues in "The Figure of the Youth as a Virile Poet," "We are concerned with the whole personality, and, in effect, we are saying that the poet who writes the heroic poem that will satisfy all these is of us and all of us in time to come, will accomplish it by the power of his reason, the force of his imagination, and, in addition, the effortless and inescapable process of his own individuality" (1954, 46). That process of personality is in *Notes* a deliberately leisurely one. "Delayed progression is wonderful here," Moore comments on some of the local effects in *Notes* (1986, 381). But she is also pointing to the delaying tactics of Stevens's characteristic ironic reserve, through which his individuality bursts to reveal the imagination as emotionally complex, committed to central principles, impatient with received aesthetic values, and thoroughly agnostic but uneasy with the unknown. The narrative, generating its powerful allegory, also allegorizes the mind that lies behind it, accreting, effect by effect, a strong sense of its presence.

The period of the composition of *Notes* was one in which Stevens was enthralled by the metaphor of the soldier and allegory of war. Stevens found the "pressure of reality," however compelling, an inadequate corrective to the fixed gaze. Consequently, his insistence at the end of *Notes* that the poet and the soldier share a noble purpose finds, in the temporal allegory of *Notes*, a meditation on process and creation that opposes the fixed image (roaring, like the lion at the "enraging desert," against silence and its own visual perception [1954, 384]) and opposes, likewise, the tyranny of the senses. Observing the importance of the poem's coda, James Longenbach argues that "the 'idea' of 'Notes Toward a Supreme Fiction' is the role of the writer in a time of war," though he qualifies this bold but narrow assertion by saying that "the poem is about a writer's purpose any time" (1991, 250). The strength of Longenbach's resultant reading is that it asserts a unity and a central purpose to the poem, detecting in it the shape of a political or social allegory, and therefore suggesting that as a poem dealing with history and society its dimensions are epic, not lyrical.

However, the structure of the poem remains undescribed, and its

allegorical outline, though it surely does contain much of political import, derives from the most elemental of sources, one that Stevens uses
with gleeful irony. *Notes* is a revisionary meditation on Genesis, which
for him is not so much a religious text as the prototype of what he describes (with regard to another poem) as the tendency of the human to
"see reflections of his self in nature" (1966, 403). The poem argues,
among other issues, that the poet's responsibility is to invent a fiction that
resists the general tendency of fictions to harden into artifacts. Of course,
all institutions are implicated here—religion foremost, but other political
and social institutions as well. The face of slate is both the face of a defunct god and the face of the poet's own fear of imagery that the eye
cannot escape. For a poet committed to the senses, a poet who, unlike
Blake, believes that the senses and the imagination are complicit, Stevens,
by the time he wrote *Notes,* has become highly suspicious of his own
imagery. The reason is that, as he says, the imagined and the real are "two
things of opposite natures," though they "depend on one another" (1954,
392). Fiction does not require us to confuse these two things, but rather
allows us to honor them both in their own spheres and in their occasional
conflation. But the fixed gaze mistakes the image for the real, mistakes
itself as the cause of whatever it beholds. Stevens mistrusts his most obvious language-gift, his painterly descriptive voice, because it does not represent the force of "nobility" but of the imagination's failure to press
"back against the pressure of reality." The lion's roar, however limited in
idea, at least protests fixity.

In addition to whatever political and social ideas it contains, the
poem is largely the narrative of Stevens's meditation on the pitfalls of the
trope as mediator between imagination and reality. The shape of the
poem, though Stevens seems to have distrusted myth, is not that of a
formal argument but of a myth creating itself, a narrative of meditation
and temporality that resists lyric self-sufficiency. *Notes Toward a Supreme
Fiction* was not the first poem Stevens conceived of in terms of myth,
rather it was the culmination of many years of critiquing and recasting
the familiar motifs of classical and Hebraic myth. Stevens's letter to Hi
Simons, quoted above, describes his poetics (with regard to the composition of "On an Old Horn") by seeming to recast Genesis in terms of
Darwin, acknowledging the poet's preoccupation with first causes:

Man sees reflections of himself in nature. Suppose we start all over again; we start as birds, say, and see reflections of ourselves in man: perhaps we were men once, or we may even become men. This occasions a toot on the horn. Incidentally, while we are changing from birds to men some queer things are likely to happen. Bird babies become men babies, with some unexpected transitional features. Just why I happened to think of the tail of a rat instead of a beak or feathers, I don't know. Perhaps, as a bird's tailfeathers vanish, they look a bit like the tail of a rat.

As the change progresses and as we begin to think the thoughts of men, there may be survivals of the thinking of our primitive state. This occasions another toot on the horn. But the things of which birds sing are probably subject to change, like the things of which men think, so that, whether bird or man, one has, after all, only one's own horn on which to toot, one's own synthesis on which to rely; one's own fortitude of spirit is the only "fester Burg"; without that fortitude one lives in chaos. . . . Suppose, now, we try the thing out, let the imagination create chaos by conceiving of it. The stars leave their places and move about aimlessly, like insects on a summer night. Now, a final toot on the horn. That is all that matters. The order of the spirit is the only music of the spheres: or rather, the only music. (1966, 403)

A key phrase here is "try the thing out." The link implicitly made between the progression of change and the necessity of narrative form suggests that "On an Old Horn"—and by implication, I would argue, *Notes* as well—is best seen as the kind of allegory Walter Benjamin has described in the work of Baudelaire, which, in Jonathan Culler's words, "identifies allegory as the semiotic mode of modern consciousness; objects of the world have become commodities that can be invested only with contingent meaning" (53). This sense of object as commodity rather than as symbol, and the sense of liberation that comes with perceiving things this new way, perceiving as a person not as an image of a person, are among the topics of "The Man on the Dump:"

> Now in the time of spring (azaleas, trilliums,
> Myrtle, viburnums, daffodils, blue phlox),
> Between that disgust and this, between the things
> That are on the dump (azaleas and so on)
> And those that will be (azaleas and so on),
> One feels the purifying change. One rejects
> The trash.
>
> That's when the moon creeps up
> To the bubbling of bassoons. That's the time
> One looks at the elephant-colorings of tires.
> Everything is shed: and the moon comes up as the moon
> (All its images are in the dump) and you see
> As a man (not like an image of a man),
> You see the moon rise in the empty sky. (1954, 202)

This characterization of the world of objects, which in *Notes* is opposed to the world of process, places Stevens precisely where he would be both amused and horrified to find himself, in the camp of the cultural Marxists.

    The passion of Stevens's rejection of the fixed gaze is not only the emotional but the aesthetic focus of the poem in that the contingency of its central figures, not their fixity, is their empowering characteristic. The unity of *Notes,* in keeping with its myth structure, is an emotional not a logical one, and the temporality it imitates, like *Paradise Lost,* is the characteristic movement of the creation and founding myth from engenderment (the poet's declaration of love for his muse, the imagination and the initial perception of the sun) through the evolution of human society to fulfillment, somewhat ironically, of civilization in the figure of the soldier, the secular hero of indeterminacy. These are the early days of Time in which humanity is inventing its relationship to its god and its own emotions, and puzzling out the relationship among imagination, perception, and reality.

Stevens planned and wrote *Notes* not as a single poem but as a sequence of thirty brief poems, plus the coda. His letter to the Cummington Press on May 14, 1942, lays out this plan in clear and confident detail (1966, 406). But poems have a way of running away with poets. The scheme Stevens imposed on his thirty poems, including his careful ordering, and the unified force of his imagination weld the sequence together in such a way as to emphasize its peculiar narrative and underscore an allegorical intention that, while I believe it is clear in the poem, may not have much to do with Stevens's original plan. Aesthetically, the poem orders itself around nonfixated imagery, troping on the tentative relationship between the senses and what they encounter. Yet the kind of imagery *Notes* rejects (though often presenting it) is the kind the New Critics take as touchstones of the poet's purpose. The restless movement from one half-generated image to another, from one unfulfilled landscape to the next, requires sympathy with an almost Blakean distrust of stasis. It is the movement of myth and is continuous, not lyric, in shape. This movement is not entirely new to Stevens, since "The Comedian as the Letter C" is a raw version of it, but it takes a challenging form in *Notes*. This myth or antimyth temporality and calculated refusal of lyric stasis accounts for the poem's air of unease, its fever to embody as well as trumpet change.

No section of this poem, however, either fully represents or renders a precis of the whole. Brief examinations of three sections, the lion in the desert ("It Must Be Abstract," V), the section in which major man, the MacCullough, replaces Adam as preeminent reimaginer of origins ("It Must Be Abstract," VIII), and the "lasting visage" section ("It Must Give Pleasure," III) illustrate some of the ways in which Stevens's myth of self-origin displaces the more ordinary kind of creation myth, and the ways in which fixity, the snake in the garden, tempts the unwary perceiver. In themselves, however, these sections are necessarily fragmentary, incomplete. The motifs they touch upon generate larger tropes of self-creation and perception to evoke "the indefinite, impersonal, atmospheres and oceans" (as he wrote in his commonplace book [33])—the varieties of *materia poetica* to which the poem's rejection of fixity refers.

The lion of "It Must Be Abstract," V, that "roars at the engaging desert" is a prototype of the artist who continually replaces one perception, one image, with another, who deliberately confounds imagery of the eye with that of the ear, and who, perhaps, imagines that in his art he makes the world in his image:

> The lion roars at the enraging desert,
> Reddens the sand with his red-colored noise,
> Defies red emptiness to evolve his match,
>
> Master by foot and jaws and by the mane,
> Most supple challenger. The elephant
> Breaches the darkness of Ceylon with blares,
>
> The glitter-goes on surfaces of tanks,
> Shattering velvetest far-away. The bear,
> The ponderous cinnamon, snarls in his mountain
>
> At summer thunder and sleeps through winter snow.
> But you, ephebe, look from your attic window,
> Your mansard with a rented piano. You lie
>
> In silence upon your bed. You clutch the corner
> Of the pillow in your hand. You writhe and press
> A bitter utterance from your writhing, dumb,
>
> Yet voluble dumb violence. You look
> Across the roofs as sigil and as ward
> And in your centre mark them and are cowed . . .
>
> These are the heroic children whom time breeds
> Against the first idea—to lash the lion,
> Caparison elephants, teach bears to juggle. (1954, 384)

The "red-colored noise" is a medium of process, not of fixity. But the lion, a creature of nature not culture, represents only one aspect of making too many different voices to describe in terms of a single personification. The elephant and bear, "the ponderous cinnamon," add their noise to the creation of a composite voice that is the only voice useful to a poet.

Instead of God creating nature, it is nature that here creates; the way these animals interact with their environment—imposing their imaginations on it, yet yielding to its imperatives—hardly contrasts with the ephebe's looking from his attic window, lying in silence upon his bed. Like the lion, elephant, and bear, the ephebe's first sound is "a bitter utterance" pressed from his "writhing, dumb, / Yet voluble dumb violence." Learning to be a poet, then, begins with instinct, with a natural need to impose oneself on one's environment. It is not a happy beginning because it is triggered by need rather than desire, and results in the ephebe's being "cowed" by his lonely speech, which still lacks form, comprehensiveness, and audience. The next step for him is to harness need, colonize nature, resist the desire to rest with the "first idea," and claim all the available voices, "lash the lion, / Caparison elephants, teach bears to juggle."

The ephebe's task, in part, is to bridge the gap between nature and culture, but this means refusing the authority of the "first idea" (that is, not denying reality but refusing to rest on an unvoiced perception of it) by giving voice and therefore names to "what is to be." The deep irony of *Notes* as a critique of the creation myth is that the self-creation of the artist results in the "death of all" gods, turning the idea of origin against itself. At the same time the ephebe must understand how vulgar this project is, how like the lion's roar and the bear's snarl. Recognizing the contingency of creation, its inextricable bond with mortality, the tentativeness of perception, the impermanence of metaphor, and the flux of the imagination requires acknowledging that the relationship between the poet and reality is a problem not to be resolved by recourse to first ideas. Thus the task of self-creation deconstructs the myth of origin and substitutes for it an ironic grounding of the poetic impulse in the sheer vulgarity of noise.

The problem of major man versus medium man haunts the poem. "It Must Be Abstract," VIII, presents the problem of housing the major man, finding a place for him on earth (like Adam, dismissed as the father of false rationality in section IV) and in reality (reconciling imagination and reality):

> Can we compose a castle-fortress-home,
> Even with the help of Viollet-le-Duc,
> And set the MacCullough there as major man?

The first idea is an imagined thing.
The pensive giant prone in violet space
May be the MacCullough, an expedient,

Logos and logic, crystal hypothesis,
Incipit and a form to speak the word
And every latent double in the word,

Beau linguist. But the MacCullough is MacCullough.
It does not follow that major man is man.
If MacCullough himself lay lounging by the sea,

Drowned in its washes, reading in the sound,
About the thinker of the first idea,
He might take habit, whether from wave or phrase,

Or power of the wave, or deepened speech,
Or a leaner being, moving in on him,
Of greater aptitude and apprehension,

As if the waves at last were never broken,
As if the language suddenly, with ease,
Said things it had laboriously spoken.

The major man, the MacCullough, a kind of Highlands stereotype, is a bully of the imagination, a figure that embodies, to some degree, in human form the first idea, and therefore is a prototype god—or satire of a god—but who resists godlike status by remaining insistently the MacCullough. However, though postulated by the collective human imagination, he is not a representative man because he is implicated in "Logos and logic, [a] crystal hypothesis," which as pensive giant he both embodies and expresses. Indeed, his own humanity prevents him from seeing himself as originator, though that role seems thrust upon him by others and even by himself. Whether the MacCullough is the same major man who was secretary of the treasury when Stevens was at Harvard (as Harold Bloom points out [1977, 213]), he is surely a figure of vast potential, requiring a "castle-fortress-home" (a phrase that embodies the history of home from the middle ages to the present), and able, perhaps, to understand language as a process, reading in the sea the history of the Adamism that haunts the human imagination, and perceiving the potential for a "possibly still more human human, a composite human" (1966, 434) that would be more representative, less a bully of imagination, less likely to mistake logos for Logos and logic, less likely to form crystal hypotheses. Thus the diminution of humans from the antediluvian world of Genesis, when those who lived close to the dream of origin survived hundreds of years and fathered or mothered hundreds of children to the more nakedly human world after the flood, finds parallel in the diminution from major man to that leaner being, less burdened with the illusions of imagined godliness, who may be the medium man who can balance imagination and reality with becoming fixated by images of gods or himself.

The face of stone in "It Must Give Pleasure," III, though "lasting," is, like Shelley's Ozymandias, a monument to a dead god and to an inadequate aesthetic, the kind that prefers fixity because it physically outlasts the artist:

> A lasting visage in a lasting bush,
> A face of stone in an unending red,
> Red-emerald, red-slitted-blue, a face of slate,
>
> An ancient forehead hung with heavy hair,
> The channel slots of rain, the red-rose-red
> And weathered and the ruby-water-worn,
>
> The vines around the throat, the shapeless lips,
> The frown like serpents basking on the brow,
> The spent feeling leaving nothing of itself,
>
> Red-in-red repetitions never going
> Away, a little rusty, a little rouged,
> A little roughened and ruder, a crown
>
> The eye could not escape, a red renown

Blowing itself upon the tedious ear.
An effulgence faded, dull cornelian

Too venerably used. That might have been.
It might and might have been. But as it was,
A dead shepherd brought tremendous chords from hell

And bade the sheep carouse. Or so they said.
Children in love with them brought early flowers
And scattered them about, no two alike.

The "visage" is only a false front, not an idea or the embodiment of an idea but the fossil of one. This is the face God hid from Cain, reconstructed by some forgotten sculptor and left adrift in the red world of lost, incomplete, or inadequate art—a red world, like the lion's red desert, a place of inadequate articulation where time, the actual First Idea that underlies this poem, has its way. The sculpture face betrays, as inadequate art tends to, an uncomfortably ambiguous relationship with nature. Its roughness is a consequence of its raw, half-made, incompletely imagined state, the failure of the artist to fully appreciate the difference between nature and culture—another idea rippling through the entire poem. The "red renown" of this face, like the lion's roar, echoes only in its own ear. It might have once been adequate for someone's need, but the Orphic ideal of poetry, a raising of voices in "tremendous chords from hell," challenged it, rendered it obsolete; and the flowers brought by children in love with sheep, a gentler kind of animal, in their fragile individuality embody a more contingent but more spontaneous and satisfying gesture than any that could be fixed in stone. Music, like the flowers, quickly fades, but that is its beauty. The fixity of the stone face indicates its bankruptcy not only as a religious symbol but as a prototype of the artist's task.

Though Exodus warns against the making of "carved images," artists have not always understood that as a warning not to let art become static. Stevens, however, sees such fixity as a reversion to the first idea, which, while hardly a wrong idea, once named becomes perverted into the idea of a god or gods and becomes the inspiration for a falsification of art and perversion of the imagination. As Stevens remarked, "One of the approaches to fiction is by way of its opposite: reality, the truth, the thing observed, the purity of the eye" (1966, 444); the fiction, however, must not attempt to *embody* truth or literal perception because then it would fail to be abstract. Nothing could be less abstract than the face of slate, and nothing further from the supreme fiction, which must give us, instead of morbidities of stone and the fixation of origins, the contingent pleasures of music and flowers.

Read as a response to or critique of Genesis, borrowing part of its narrative force from the continuous overturning of motifs from that vast myth of origin, much of the rest of its force derived from the temporal allegory of meditation that orders and paces the sections, *Notes* achieves sufficient wholeness of structure and purpose to suggest how central to the imagination is the generation of ideas or myths of creation. One of the essential shaping distinctions of the poem is that the imaginer is different from the image—and recognizing this illuminates the larger symmetry implied by the "circle spread / To the final full." The supreme fiction, whatever it may be, requires a large imagining to perceive it. Moore herself, in "Marriage," "A Grave," and other important poems had drawn fairly large circles herself, and the ease with which she enters Stevens's poetic vision may indicate an important difference between the high modernists of her own generation and a later generation of poets struggling in their shadow. The poets of a later generation would require a decade or more of effort before breaking out of their narrowly focused poetic and attempting work on the scale of *Notes Toward a Supreme Fiction*. Only with the appearance of ambitious sequences like Berryman's *Dream Songs* and Lowell's *History* would the poets of the following generation attain a vision comparable to the ambition, aesthetic largess, and imaginative requirements of Stevens's elephantine and elephant-colored fiction.

Williams & Moore

History and the Colloquial Style

After Browning and Tennyson, any tendency of poets to disregard history and temporality as subjects, shaping forces, or even rhetorical strategies would seem regressive. Eliot and Pound, both born in Frederick Jackson Turner's frontier country, rejected the idea of American exceptionalism and turned to English and European historical and cultural traditions, though with some degree of skepticism, while the poets who remained in America found history a more generally problematic issue. Further, these poets were faced with the problem that the American language in its spoken rhythms and written idioms no longer conformed to the usage honored in textbooks of philology, although much of the magazine verse of the early part of the twentieth century seemed archaic in its longings for a pure British lyricism. William Carlos Williams and Marianne Moore represent distinct but complementary attempts to utilize the American accent in verse, independent of the familiar metrics of Sidney, Tennyson, and Longfellow. And Williams with his calculated rejection of history—which is actually a way of redirecting its imperatives toward his own aesthetic needs—offers the most individual attempt to reconsider the very rhetoric in which history is generally cast.

In the American Grain

"We arc deceived by history," William Carlos Williams warns in an essay ironically entitled "The Virtues of History" (1925, 197). Williams, though antihistoricist, was drawn to the imaginative possibilities of history as much as he was repelled by its insistence on "generic patterns" and its conformity to "mere accidents of geography and climate" (1951, 171; 1925, 188). He was dismayed by what he saw as an aesthetic as well as a moral issue, one that in speaking particularly of America he defined as history's "nearly universal lack of scale" (1925, 75). Perhaps consequently, Williams is preoccupied in nearly all of his verse with scale, which is closely linked to measure and rhythm. To explore the imaginative dimensions of history and avoid the positivist or determinist theories in vogue in the early part of this century, he offers an aesthetic critique of history true to his pragmatic temperament and worldview, one derived from his commitment to craft as "an embodiment of knowledge." His writings about history, from the prose epic *In the American Grain* to the protean collage epic *Paterson,* reject historical positivism in handling documentary material and instead existentially embrace the drama, rhetoric, and artifacts of history to fuel a finely textured vision of the present.

In this discussion "March" and "History" provide the major examples of Williams's early stance toward history and demonstrate his fascination with the artifact; but more than that, they point to his early willingness to fracture conventional genre, unravel ordinary rhetoric, and reject the established privilege of form in favor of a poetic of his own devising. "History," in particular, centers its poetic in consciousness by imitating the movement of the mind. Although fragmented and collage-like, this poem relies on an organizing principle that anticipates *Paterson* and parallels (without imitating) important developments in contemporary European poetry, which had been shattered by war, the exhaustion of tradition, and the earliest discoveries by Freud and Jung of the power, arbitrariness, and will-toward-order of the unconscious.

The diary-like language of *In the American Grain* illuminates the rhetorical motives of the author in the context of an experimental revisionist history. Williams approaches those historical personages who in his view had been incorrectly perceived and remakes them in his own image. As he says about Aaron Burr, "He's there in history as you design him. / He's in myself and so I dig through lines to resurrect him" (1925, 197). So thoroughly do the consciousness and point of view of the speaker empower the writing that it becomes difficult for the reader to reimage these same events in a more detached narrative. This goes beyond empathy. In a self-revealing passage at the opening of "The Founding of Quebec," Williams asserts the immanence of Champlain in the present tense of the poet's aesthetic, entertaining an absolute identification of author and subject in the common ground of the text: "Here *is* a man after my own heart. Is it merely in a book? So am I then, merely in a book. You see? Here at last I find the thing I love. I mean here *is* the thing, accurately, my own world, the world in which I myself breathe and walk and live—against that which you present" (1925, 167).

Though Williams resists his own transcendent subjectivity by claiming that he and Champlain "live in different worlds," it is clear that even to perceive the existence of those worlds—separate or congruous—requires self-consciousness, not an archaeological objectivity. He prefers a "pageant of wild beasts" to a scholarly calm, since history "lives in us practically day by day," and therefore "we should fear it"; though history and tradition, most vitally, form a "fountain" at which we, the occupants of the present, may refresh ourselves (1925, 188–89). Emphatically, history is not a set of values or a living aesthetic but is a source on which the imagination may draw.

It follows that Williams, in a long line of romantics, values imagination more than artifacts (despite his much-quoted "no ideas but in things"). However, the interplay between these poles suggests to him a particular approach to history, one more properly designated as aesthetic rather than as social or political. As Williams said in recalling his early development, he was "interested in the construction of an image before the image was popular in poetry" (1958, 21). While this retrospective comment probably implies more deliberation in his enterprise than he brought to it at the time, the aesthetic struggles of his early poems incorporate a good deal of intellectual exploration. Rather than theorizing, however, Williams subjected his materials to the crucible of poetic immediacy, bending abstract concerns to an aesthetic will.

"March"

Williams's process of constructing images derives from his phenomenological approach to his materials, most notably in his use of the artifacts and temporal constructs of history. But he approaches these materials with the cool detachment with which Saussure approached the sign. Separating the artifact (which ontologically functions as a symbol, a literary device Williams deprecated) from the cultural and social concepts it represents, he argues that history survives not in material objects but only through correlation with the life before us. In "March," first published in 1916, the tenacity of winter (as well as something monumental about it that's left undescribed) reminds the speaker of the persistence of artifacts:

> March,
> you remind me of
> the pyramids, our pyramids—
> stript of the polished stone
> that used to guard them!
>   March,
> you are like Fra Angelico
> at Fiesole, painting on plaster! (1986, 137–38)

The Keatsian excess of this metaphor deepens when Williams self-consciously links the immediate temporal situation (late winter) with geographically remote relics (pyramids, frescoes). The lingering seasonal chill becomes an embodiment of youthful creativity, and reminds us that art in our own era occurs under particular conditions, usually discouraging, and for personal rather than social reasons:

> March,
> you are like a band of
> young poets that have not learned
> the blessedness of warmth
> (or have forgotten it).
> At any rate—
> I am moved to write poetry
> for the warmth there is in it
> and for the loneliness—
> a poem that shall have you
>   in it March.

By juxtaposing pyramids and frescoes (art as a social imperative) with the band of young poets (art as personal imperative), Williams distinguishes between the contemporary creative urge and the universality of art. And although he uses March as a trope, he also rejects the ex-

hausted tradition of seasonal metaphor. Rather than generating a particularized body of association derived from the actual characteristics of winter (cold, renewal, and lengthening days), March reminds Williams of old
and deteriorated artworks, and personified becomes a gang of unsuccessful poets. The similes strip March of its tactile reality and replace it with
a string of associations too personal to privilege their source with the
authority of origin. That is, nothing about March except, marginally, its
chill, generates this particular string of associations. The arbitrariness of
this simile-making seems to cheer the speaker. But severing the link between vehicle and tenor carries grave implications, since it undermines
the connotative values by which the language of poetry has usually con-
veyed its complexities.

In a talk in 1948 Williams explained that "the subject matter of the
poem is always phantasy—what is wished for, realized in the 'dream' of
the poem—but . . . the structure confronts something else" (1954, 281).
That "something else" is the image, the material of conventional metaphor and symbol, the signifier to which Williams consigns all reality, al-
lotting no substance to the signified. That is, although the subject matter
directs the poem, the text is made out of signifiers not out of phantasy.
The purpose of the imagination is to generate a text, not to transcend
language. This insistence on the material limitations of language and poetry distinguishes him from much of romanticism, in which reality is at
least as manifest in the "glory and dream" as in the landscape that inspirits
the vision. Williams doesn't reject the dream, which he sees as Freudian
wish-fulfillment; but he is determined to avoid confusing it with the
exterior world. He resolutely denies all confounding of the I and the
Not-I. For him distinctions are definitive, and the distinction between
the dream and the world is particularly important.

Committed to a highly visual but nonsymbolic poetic, Williams
must not merely present but must reintegrate the artifact in the world,
masking its museum smell, revitalizing history through the immediacy of
the quotidian. His poetic so emphasizes the mirroring of fact that it sometimes becomes more mimetic than expressive, despite the rather numb
assertions of *Spring and All*. The insistence on the poem as a made object
further distinguishes him from the more vatic romantics he imitates in his
earliest poems, and lends a deliberation to his meditations on language
that leads to an irony no poet-prophet would care to entertain for long.

Vatic romantics look to transcend language, but, as Williams suggests in
Paterson, to replicate the extinction of language in the ineffable is to make
an effigy of oneself—saintly, perhaps, but artificial:

> The language cascades into the
> invisible, beyond and above: the falls
> of which it is the visible part—
>
> Not until I have made of it a replica
> will my sins be forgiven and my
> disease cured—in wax. (1992, 145)

The crowning irony is that the poem itself, divorced from the "phantasy" it cannot possibly embody, becomes an artifact, a vehicle with no
empowering tenor, an act of mimesis that so completely rejects everything expressive that it no longer embodies the poet's life but only a
waxen (and asexual) replica. The note of despair so frequently (and so
vitally) in *Paterson* associated with the urgency of sex results from Williams's
acknowledgment of this self-imposed dilemma:

> This is my direction. Whither? I
> cannot say. I cannot say
> more than how. The how (howl) only
> is at my disposal (proposal): watching—
> colder than stone.
>
>   a bud forever green,
> tight-curled, upon the pavement, perfect
> in juice and substance but divorced, divorced
> from its fellows, fallen low—
>   .   Divorce is
> the sign of knowledge in our time,
> divorce, divorce! (1992, 17)

Extending this language-consciousness to distinguish artifact per se from
history as a quotidian force (a fountain) is a central tactic in *Paterson,* but
Williams uses this strategy much earlier in his career.

"History"

"History," published in *Poetry* in 1917 and immediately reprinted in *Al Que Quiere!,* juxtaposes the domesticity of a Sunday at the museum and a walk in the park with historical artifacts and natural imagery of ascending challenge to his poetic, which here relies on his newly invented tactic of collage. In 1917, before Dada was well known in America, this collage technique represented a clean break with the visionary-romantic poetic he briefly embraced as a novice but, perhaps realizing that this wasn't really the poetic of his idol Keats, almost immediately he outgrew it. Many of the poems in *Al Que Quiere!* imitate the public discourse of a politician or soapbox orator. But the speaker of "History" is bemused and wandering, and even when he addresses a second person seems to follow no logic but that of association or metonymy. The poem traces acts of perception and mediation rather than narrative, and adheres to the interior voice rather than to the rhetoric of persuasion that empowers poems like "Tract" or "Gulls." "History" does conclude with a note of persuasion, but the bulk of the poem makes no attempt to prepare for this closing exhortation, since it, too, is a product of metonymy rather than logic.

The poem opens by distinguishing the speaker in the domestic land-scape from the natural artifact separated by its otherness:

> A wind might blow a lotus petal
> over the pyramids—but not this wind.
>
> Summer is a dried leaf.
>
> Leaves stir this way then that
> on the baked asphalt, the wheels
> of motor cars rush over them,—
>   gas smells mingle with leaf smells. (1986, 81)

Whatever occurs in Egypt has nothing to do with what happens here, the poet notes. The wind does not represent all winds, is not a symbol, an archetype, or a metaphor but merely one fact among many. Yet the synec-doche "Summer is a dried leaf" represents the sort of rhetoric that makes larger figurative assertions possible. Curbing the universalizing tendencies of tropes of various kinds while admitting their immediate use is the generative strategy of this poem. Williams allows his figures only as much vitality as they can command in the immediacy of their setting. Summer can be a dried leaf only because the figure is so reductive. In this withered state the figure can speak to the desolation Williams tries to depict, a compounding of the brutally mechanical city scene with the more remote and somewhat irrelevant worlds of history and nature. His ironic angle of vision confounds the museumgoers with the objects they have come to "worship": "Simpering clay-fetish faces counting / through the turnstile." Indeed, the speaker has come to "mingle," to empathize with the life that generates these artifacts, then in his meditation to precipitate the artifacts from life.

In the second section the speaker confronts the sarcophagus of Uresh-Nai, a priest entombed for 6,000 years in an object that represents nothing but the arrogance that initiated it. The tomb is a flawless work of art, yet all attempts to inculcate it with meaning, with "phantasms" like love, fail because of the plain materiality of the tomb and the corpse within:

> But love is an oil to embalm the body.
> Love is a packet of spices, a strong-
> smelling liquid to be squirted into
> the thigh. No?

The coy voice courts dissent. No indeed: love is none of this. Insulated behind his high walls, the priest conceals from himself the central flaw in his scheme, which is his unexamined faith in the efficacy of the artwork as living symbol. Thus the sarcophagus, now an historical artifact, represents his character flaws, his arrogance and presumption, rather than embodying the love, immortality, and the appetites he treasured in life. The stone has in a way "taken up his spirit," but it remains stone nonetheless.

The third section addresses the fallen priest and encourages him to soliloquize from his own epitaph, suggesting that language itself retains a kind of life, since the granite has "held [these figures] / with so soft a hand the while [his] own flesh has been fifty times / through the guts of oxen." From Keats, Williams learned not only that the products of the imagination offer a vision of indestructibility but also that this vision cannot adequately substitute for reality. As the "Ode on a Grecian Urn" suggests, the difference between art and life is as absolute as that between the image and the abstraction, between reality and "phantasy." The epitaph itself endures, and the priest, if he could read it, would find its vitality renewed by the act of reading. The reader, in the flush of life, might believe that love, the greatest abstraction, endures even longer than granite, but such endurance cannot help the oxen-devoured priest.

In the fourth section the priest again soliloquizes, arguing for the survival of love in his person, but he can only invoke lust, the memory of flesh. Because his own flesh has turned to stone (whatever part of it hasn't passed through oxen) he hasn't learned to distinguish himself from the artifact that he supposed intimately represents him; he asserts that in it he thrives, still capable of love, still available to nakedness and beauty. Recalling the fleeting pleasures of sex and the insatiable desires of the spirit, he speaks with the phallic vanity of stone, not the timidity of flesh:

> "Here I am with head high and a
> burning heart eagerly awaiting
> your caresses, whoever it may be,
> for granite is not harder than
> my love is open, runs loose among you!
>
> I arrogant against death! I
> who have endured! I worn against
> the years!"

The priest's soliloquies, celebrating sensuality, are poems of grandeur and high pretense, as indicated by their elevated levels of diction. For the priest, art means salvation in the most literal and palpable sense. When in the year of his choosing "the lid shall be lifted" he will "walk about the temple / and breathe the air of the place," as if merely waking from a long nap. This is not the sort of life-giving quality we can reasonably accord the work of art. The priest has failed to apprehend the distinction between phantasy and reality. The level of unreality rises in the second soliloquy when the priest argues that love will outlast even granite. On sentimental grounds we might be tempted to accede to this, since surely as a value love has a long and convincing history. But this second soliloquy argues for the survival of the sexual love Marvell and other masters of the carpe diem tradition have warned us cannot rise from the grave:

> "My flesh is turned to stone. I
> have endured my summer. The flurry
> of falling petals is ended. Lay
> the finger upon this granite. I was
> well desired and fully caressed
> by many lovers but my flesh
> withered swiftly and my heart was
> never satisfied. Lay your hands
> upon the granite as a lover lays his
> hand upon the thigh and upon the
> round breasts of her who is beside
> him, for now I will not wither,
> now I have thrown off secrecy, now
> I have walked naked into the street,
> now I have scattered my heavy beauty
> in the open market."

Williams flatly refuses this transcendental absolute, the equation of subject and object, the denial of difference. While the survival of love as a value may not be in question, the priest believes his tomb can embody that survival. He expects it to function as an avatar rather than merely as an emblem of his departed lust and his dedication to the Sky Goddess. This farfetched negation of death represents a superstitious perversion of art, wholly unsuitable to Williams's present-tense aesthetic of material immediacy. Williams respects the imagination eternalized by Uresh-Nai's faith in immortality, but he's too aware of the difference between life and art to accept the artifact as a conquest of reality or death.

Blurring that distinction generates an error of consequence: the perversion of religion for the sake of personal satisfaction. The long-dead priest, "With head high and a / burning heart," anticipates the resumption of his lustful career, but his arrogance in the face of death is empty bravado. What has survived is the imaginative vision that enabled him to postulate this theoretical overthrow of death. In its way, it is a noble vision, but in Williams's quotidian world it seems laughable. "History" is disrespectful of religious and aesthetic traditions; as Williams argues in *Paterson,* the poem must make a new truth not merely rehash the old ones:

> and the craft,
> subverted by thought, rolling up, let
> him beware lest he turn to no more than
> the writing of stale poems . . .
> Minds like beds always made up,
>   (more stony than a shore)
> unwilling or unable. (1992, 4–5)

To counter what he sees as patent nonsense, Williams invites us in the fifth section of "History" to walk in the park "while the day lasts." Life, we are sententiously reminded, "is good." The solemnly respectful nod to the carpe diem tradition only reminds us how distinctly Williams foils this and other expectations with his insistence on the inefficacy and pretense of conventional metaphor, how tenaciously he argues for a poetry of the American present:

> Look! this
> northern scenery is not the Nile, but—
> these benches—the yellow and purple dusk—
> the moon there—these tired people—
> the lights on the water!

In this melodramatic appeasement of reality the persistence of the metaphor-making passion for linking and entwining unrelated images again asserts itself, almost against the poet's will. He must agree that if the people in the dusk resemble "Jews and—Ethiopians," that the world indeed is young and "colored like—a girl that has come / upon / a lover!" But suspicious of this easy sentiment, he concludes by asking skeptically and rhetorically "Will that do?" This renewal of the affections, however uneasily regarded in this instance, in the quotidian world does "do" for Williams in poem after poem, often through highly conventional seasonal imagery ("The Widow's Lament in Springtime," "Burning the Christmas Greens"), often, as in this poem, by ironically juxtaposing the inert artifact with the organic imagery of ordinary life.

The concluding and conclusive dismissal of the past in "History" requires American art to reject tradition—of which America has little anyway—disrespect history, and center itself in the exertions and consciousness of the contemporary artist. As the speaker of "The Men" argues:

> Wherein is Moscow's dignity
> more than Passaic's dignity?
> A few men have added color better
> to the canvas, that's all. (1986, 278)

That is, Russian tradition lends to its art "color" (perhaps red, in this instance) but not the more efficacious "dignity," and the achievements of a few good artists can surely be matched in America. Dignity, an abstraction, is what Williams calls the phantasy, the proper subject—or perhaps inspiration—of poetry, while color, though Williams values it, is a local effect. Though resolutely visual and tactile in his language, Williams nonetheless longs for the abstract, partly because it is independent of the limitations of facts, the accidents of history. "The Men" goes on to point out those limitations:

> The river is the same
> the bridges are the same
> there is the same to be discovered
> of the sun—

But the poets who confront these facts bring to the scene the phantasy that changes facts, makes them into art, makes them the "news" that he notes in a later poem is "difficult / to get" and yet so essential that, as "The Men" notes, it changes those who learn of it by more clearly individualizing them, better distinguishing them from each other:

> Only,
> the men are different who see it

draw it down in their minds
or might be different.

This differing among men and minds recalls Williams's self-conscious confrontation with Champlain. Defining ourselves and distinguishing artifact from mind and mind from minds may be difficult, but such ontological arts are necessary. American art will flourish when the American artist recognizes the autonomy of the mind, stops bemoaning in Jamesian fashion the landscape's lack of "color," and invents an idiom appropriate to a clearsighted world freed of dogged adhesion to the past.

Two Worlds

Denying the efficacy of immutable aesthetic and religious traditions and historically empowered landscapes reinforces Williams's dismissal of linguistic assumptions. In refusing the privileged relationship of tenor to vehicle in conventional metaphor Williams undermines not only the artifactual significance of history but also the role of tradition in the arts. When Williams complained that the publication of *The Waste Land* "gave the poem back to the academics" (1951, 146), he meant that Eliot had endorsed those readers who insist on a predetermined and immutable link between the past and the present. Eliot's apparent acknowledgment of this link (in "Tradition and the Individual Talent") seemed to refute not only Williams's assertion of aesthetic independence but his program for an American language and culture.

To found his program on the insignificance of historical artifacts and the futility of the language of history seems less radical if we note that Williams acknowledges that language, in limited circumstances, is a potent—even determinant—metaphor of human vitality. History, after all, is a "fountain," a vital source at which we may replenish our sense and sensibilities. Williams in "History" seems to equate the general subject of history with positivism, which collapses under the pressure of pragmatic, consciousness-centered perception; yet in the end the past, appropriately invoked, makes possible his assertion that yes, the world is young, perpetually young, and that through the contemplation of the exhausted artifact we discover in ourselves the vitality of the present. Tradition, he admits, is "the better part of us," but art has to revitalize tradition by putting it to use, not merely by paying its respects: "Facts remain but what is the truth?" he asks (1925, 189). Later, Williams would suggest that of the "two worlds" we inhabit—the first the world of memory and history, the second that of the quotidian—it is the latter that offers "things the imagination feeds upon," those that "startle us anew" (1962, 152). For lack of this renewal through imagination, not for lack of traditional knowledge, "men die miserably every day" (1962, 161).

In "History" and other early poems Williams's phenomenological aesthetic, in dismantling the special relationship with the past that poetry has commonly assumed, discovers an alternate way of looking at the world at large, a way of defending the poet against the insistence of history and tradition. It is an aesthetic of irony that distances the abstractions that empower his intellect at the expense of his consciousness and threaten to overwhelm his poems in sentiment, the assertion of disembodied illuminations. Further, instead of relying heavily on metaphor, Williams develops the parataxis that he will later use effectively in *Paterson*. Though the closure of "History" reluctantly embraces a baldly sentimental vitality, it does not merely invoke but generates this source of energy, and therefore originates rather than merely inherits its emotional content. If that emotional content seems a little naive it is all the more American for it. "History," whatever its flaws, directs us to the major issues with which the poet would wrestle in his later work: the interplay of history with personal memory and the domestic sublime, the function of the artifact, the inefficacy and limits of metaphor, and the need to shape new rhetorical strategies to cope with a radically particularized language and vision.

Extraliterary Voices

While the problem of history generated a certain stance toward his material, Williams was even more concerned with the problem of freeing American poetry from the genre demands inherited from English and American poetry of the previous century. Other poets also addressed this issue, but Williams and Marianne Moore generated some of the most original responses to the issue. Experiments and innovations in voice and address are especially prominent in their work during the 1920s. In their attempt to shed the timeworn conventions of the lyric and monologue, including syllable-stress metrics, rhyme, stilted diction, and familiar stanza patterns, both poets draw upon the language, syntax, and to some extent the structure of extraliterary modes of expression that promise greater incisiveness, brevity, or precision than found in more derivative verse. By extraliterary I don't necessarily refer to voices that had never been heard in literature but rather those that did not derive from the established and ubiquitous voices of then-contemporary poetry, the voices Moore and Williams might reasonably have felt represented the most readily available modes of expression. Williams's apprentice imitation of these established modes produced poems "full of inversions of phrase, the rhymes inaccurate, the forms stereotype" (1951, 107), while Moore was cautious from the start and avoided publishing her early Pre-Raphaelite-like poems.

To distinguish an extraliterary voice I must first define a literary one. Mostly simply, a literary voice is one that speaks in any of the modes of poetic diction, tone, and pronominal usage readily available and common in a given era. This voice would be one a reader in that era would readily associate with poetry or verse. For example, in our own time the pronominal second-person poem invokes a now well-established literary voice, one that has a predictable range of reference, characteristically plain syntax, and sometimes a patently artificial tone of assumed intimacy. The epilogue to this study examines one such poem in detail, Robert Pinsky's "Long Branch, New Jersey." In the first three decades of this century many varieties of literary voices had established themselves; but although Williams and Moore in their earliest work tried many of these voices they rejected contemporary models and invented voices that had in common an immediacy and colloquial flexibility, yet reflected differing conceptions of the possibilities and tasks of modern poetry.

Like Wordsworth working on the same problem 120 years before, Moore and Williams had to distance themselves from the formal conventions of their era, which in the 1910s and early 1920s was still dominated by the Edwardian and Georgian poets who flourished in the literary journals. At any given time, in attempting to escape the dominant literary voices of their era, the best poets are likely to extend their range of voice into the extraliterary, as Wordsworth, Browning, and Whitman attempted to do by claiming for the brief poem the full dialogic range of discourse, as had the epic, sacred text, and novel. While Moore and Williams followed procedures and purposes common to several generations of poets attempting to renew the language, they arrived at almost opposite ends of the formal spectrum from each other, Williams committed to the illusion of randomness and dislocation, or alternately of the apparent simplicity of the prose paragraph, Moore to the imposition of a seemingly rigid order through the rigor of syllabic verse. But as Bonnie Costello has pointed out, their differences aren't easily characterized:

> On the surface Williams seems the more radical of the two poets, but one might speculate from remarks in their prose and correspondence that a submerged pattern of motives existed beneath the expressed ones, in which Williams can be seen as the initially tamer mind, constantly struggling (with brilliant flashes of success) to let the lion out and Moore can be seen as the wilder, more effusive spirit constantly trying to harness itself into communicability and acceptability. (65)

Moore gave voice to personal and even private registers of diction and adopted the tone and language of rebuke (even sometimes to address inanimate objects), the intimacy of the letter, or the matter-of-fact tone and syntax of the textbook of natural history or geography. Williams also borrowed these or comparable voices, but, like Whitman to some extent, he was equally attracted by the public voice, the politician speaking to a crowd, the editorialist (in "Impromptu: The Suckers"), the voices of women ("Portrait of a Woman in Bed," "The Widow's Lament in Springtime"), or other voices distinctly not the poet's musing in self-contained lyric monologism.

Williams and Moore by no means saw themselves as greatly similar in aesthetic outlook, though they tried to maintain sympathy and interest in each other's work. Celeste Goodridge has traced the reservations in Moore's early interest and apparent approval of Williams's work, and linked it to her later disapprobation of *Paterson,* 4. But a poet's avowed aesthetic stance, as Moore noted with regard to Williams, does not always adequately describe the poetry. Williams claimed to want no mask between the speaker of his poems and his audience, but every speech-act requires a point of view, and every point of view in a poem, shaped by the dialogic requirements of discourse, assumes the voice of an identifiable persona, exposed by function yet masked by the limitations of fiction. Moore and Williams differ in important ways, yet both their differences and their similarities reveal their attempts to solve comparable aesthetic problems.

In an early essay (1925) Williams acknowledges this strategic freshness in Moore and emphasizes the inclusiveness of her verse, its refusal of conventional poetic devices, its capacity for argument, and its rhetorical (though Williams, as Moore noted, resists this word) ease:

> Without effort Miss Moore encounters the affairs which concern her as one would naturally in reading or upon a walk outdoors. . . . Her own rhythm is particularly revealing. It does not interfere with her progress; it is the movement of the animal, it does not put itself first and ask the other to follow.
>
> * * *
>
> She occupies the thought to the end, and goes on— without connectives. . . . The essence is not broken, nothing is injured. . . . In the best modern verse, room has been made for the best of modern thought and Miss Moore thinks straight.
>
> * * *
>
> Only the most modern work has attempted to do without *ex machina* props of all sorts, without rhyme, assonance, the feudal master beat, the excuse of "nature," of the spirit, mysticism, religiosity, "love," "humor," "death." . . . Work such as Miss Moore's holds its bloom today not by using slang, not by its moral abandon or puritanical steadfastness, but by the aesthetic pleasure engendered where pure craftsmanship joins hard surface skillfully. (1970, 315)

Williams speaks here for his own aspirations, and finds in Moore some of the qualities he attributes to all the best modern poetry—including, of course, his own. Acknowledgment of her seemingly natural encounter with subject matter, her invention of a personal rhythm, and the purposeful unity of her poetry's movement must have pleased Moore. These are qualities that in her reviews, in her own language, she praises in the work of Williams and others. Moore does not concern herself to such a degree with being modern; certainly, she was not so programmatic about excluding particular technical devices from her verse, though Williams's description of her language as an act of craft must have been especially gratifying to her.

Neither poet dwells on the other's most obvious challenges to accepted poetic practice, those thematic and formal characteristics some reviewers found eccentric: Moore's elaborate syllabic stanzas, Williams's stark, at times almost telegraphic free verse, Moore's sometimes harsh social commentary, and Williams's fixation on urban minutiae. Instead, each discovers in the other's work a common interest in modern poetry as an essentially rhetorical experiment, one driven by a rage to stifle dreary poeticisms and render, as Williams put it, "a perfectly definite handling of the materials with a given intention to relate them in a certain way—a handling that is intensely, intentionally selective" (1970, 314).

The enlargement of rhetorical possibilities is the focal point of Moore's poetics. Reviewing E.E. Cummings's *XLI Poems,* Moore claims that his work is "fanciful, yet faithful to that verisimilitude of eye and of rhetoric which is so important in poetry" (1986, 125). And in a 1921 review of *Kora in Hell* she chastises Williams for attempting to deny the importance of rhetoric and its centrality to his own poetics:

> Dr. Williams' wisdom, however, is not absolute and he is sometimes petulant.
>
> "Nowadays poets spit upon rhyme and rhetoric," he says. His work provides examples of every rhetorical principle insisted on by rhetoricians and one wonders upon what ground he has been able to persuade himself that poets spit upon rhyme? Possibly by rhetoric, he means balderdash; in this case, then, we are merely poorer by one, of proofs of for his accuracy. (1986, 59)

Because Moore would not "spit upon" any usable poetic strategy or device, she reasonably questions whether Williams's pejorative use of "rhetoric" includes the various syntactical arrangements and persuasive discourses he uses to advantage in his own work—those devices and strategies that practically define rhetoric as the term is generally understood. The pragmatism of Moore represents a distinct approach to the problems of modern poetry. Her dislike of dogma reveals itself in "To a Steam Roller," in which the polemical subject excludes even the possibility of a meliorating emblem—the butterfly—and leads the speaker into a conclusion charged with exasperation. In her review she mildly expresses a comparable exasperation with Williams. Like the subject of the steamroller, he has allowed dogma as well as impatience, overstatement, and fondness for the language of manifesto to distort his own poetic practice, which by the early 1920s had begun to reach toward a full grasp of the imagination through acute observation, a wide rhetorical range, and accurate delineation of both imagery and ideas.

Williams's reply acknowledges the truth of Moore's criticism, but reminds her that his target is actually not rhetoric but slack and lifeless language:

> I cannot object to rhetoric, as you point out, but I must object to the academic associations with which rhetoric is hung and which vitiate all its significance by making the piece of work to which it is applied a dry bone. And so I have made the mistake of abusing the very thing I most use. The same with rhyme: who can object to rhyme except in the sense of the pendulum's swing against it brought about by stupid usage? I thank you for calling attention to these inaccuracies. (1957, 52)

In fact, it is Williams's innovations in rhetoric that I find most persuasive and interesting in his poetry, especially his tropes of protest, argument, and inarticulateness, and his seemingly inexhaustible tropes of persuasion, which lie at the heart of the classical definition of rhetoric. Williams has earned deserved praise for his imagery, but he is as much a poet of overt persuasion—even of a kind of editorialism—as of pictorialism. His visual aesthetic owes more to Keats than to the painters and photographers he clearly admired but who offered only the vaguest analogies to the language-acts Williams struggled to render on the page. But even that imagery, in the force of Williams's rhetoric, serves the purpose of argument. One of his central strategies, that of shaping an argument through the shifting of images, surely derives from the practice of Keats, as in the opening of "Portrait of the Author," a poem Moore particularly admired:

> The birches are mad with green points
> the wood's edge is burning with their green,
> burning, seething—No, no, no.
> The birches are opening their leaves one
> by one. Their delicate leaves unfold cold
> and separate, one by one. Slender tassels
> hang swaying from the delicate branch tips—
> Oh, I cannot say it. There is no word. (1986, 172)

Characteristically, this imagery reinforces and parallels a plainly articulated argument about the trials of authorship and its tendency to separate the poet from other people and from the things of the world. But all language-acts contain some sort of argument. More specifically, Williams is preeminently a poet of argument as a rhetorical mode, and it is the insistence, the humor, the flexibility, and the range of his argumentative voice—a range that suggests a careful reading of Browning—in poems such as "Impromptu: the Suckers," "Wind of the Village," "Struggle of Wings," and the entirety of *Spring and All* that distinguish him from the other poets of his era. To insist, as some critics have, that his formal innovations derive primarily from his contact with cubism, rapid transit, Charles Sheeler, or Alfred Stieglitz is to overlook the intimate connection between form and rhetoric, and to obscure the differences between language and other aesthetic media. Robert Lowell shrewdly reminds us that "Williams has said that he uses the forms he does for quick changes of tone, atmosphere, and speed. This makes him dangerous and difficult to imitate, because most poets have little change of tone, atmosphere, and speed in them" (1987, 41). These changes are rhetorical tactics, and studying Williams's cultural context, his relationship to Charles Sheeler, or his anatomy textbooks may provide us with interesting metaphors or analogs to these strategies, but will not help as much as direct study of the poems themselves.

Moore, as complex and cunning an artist as Williams, also is often argumentative or persuasive. But her arguments, unlike those of Will-

iams, even while she explores psychological ambiguities and the politics
of voice (in the manner of Eliot), adhere so precisely to the outlines of
external forces (often for the purpose of mocking them) that the subject,
rather than the speaker's interior stance, often shapes the rhetoric of the
poem. Typically, the central metaphor derives from a characteristic of the
external subject rather than from some objective correlative for the speaker's
emotional state, and this metaphor determines the entire rhetorical tenor
of the poem. "To a Steam Roller" is typical of several poems of the early
1920s that extend the imperative of the "I-you" interlocutor-relationship
into the realm of personal invective:

> The illustration
> is nothing to you without the application.
>   You lack half wit. You crush all the particles down
>   into close conformity, and then walk back and forth
>   on them.
>
> Sparkling chips of rock
> are crushed down to the level of the parent block.
>   Were not "impersonal judgments in aesthetic
>   matters, a metaphysical impossibility," you
>
> might fairly achieve
> it. As for butterflies, I can hardly conceive
>   of one's attending upon you, but to question
>   the congruence of the complement is vain, if it
>   exists. (1924, 21)

The impersonality of the steamroller is that of the leveler, the person who would crush rock itself back into the earth, back to its origin, so
that he could walk without effort or discomfort. The limits of his intelligence define themselves not by lack of wit, which would at least prevent
his intellectual abuse, but by obsession with utility, the great modernist
heresy. The impersonality he advocates is so powerful (and perhaps so
attractive) a force it almost seems plausible enough to nullify the truism
cited from Lawrence Gilman. That butterflies, the random beauties of
nature, would shun this person seems obvious enough, but the final sen-

tence problematizes the poem's allegorical construction by acknowledging that the possibility of butterfly and steamroller meeting is an awkward mix of figuration. Because the speaker cannot actually conceive of it she cannot judge the appropriateness of the pairing. For her, as well, the "illustration / is nothing . . . without the application"; allegory requires development and consistency, but the subject resists it. To impose on the subject a trope of mindless force and willful ignorance is one thing, but to extend the figuration beyond a certain point without violating its integrity, revealing it as a trope, is almost impossible. Yet the limits of the simple allegory define the limits of the actual subject as much as of the rhetorical strategy. Because the butterfly will never attend upon the steamroller there's no need to pursue the issue. Unable but under no requirement to resolve so outlandish a clash of rhetorical devices, the poem ends on a note of disdain. The rhetorical effect is doubly powerful; the speaker refuses her own chosen figure of delicacy and grace by conceding that the mere presence of the steamroller renders the butterfly figure so improbable that the imagination abandons it in exasperation, not at its own resources but with the subject. Proceeding from rational exposition through ironic quotation to a rhetorical crux of exasperation, the poem illustrates the dominance of the subject by allowing it to crush even the possibility of a competing, contrasting figure, conceding that such opposition in this context is too problematic. So the speaker allows the steamroller to shape the poem's closure by thoroughly exasperating her and driving from the poem all competing or temporizing language; but the very failure of the butterfly to compete as a viable trope of beauty, randomness, and nonutility illustrates how limited, ungracious, and artificial is the steamroller-person, and how insensitive to the poem's central irony.

    In "Brilliant Sad Sun" Williams also extends and tests the I-You dynamic. But here the speaker stands at some distance from a woman who, he argues, lacks both the common vitality of the waitress in Lee's Lunch and the more refined yet equally vital virtuosity of Patti "on her first concert tour." "What are your memories," he asks, "beside that purity," the act of ablution of pouring "clear water . . . from a glass pitcher"? The addressed woman's "romantic but true" thoughts seem inadequate in this context of changing seasons and blossoming appetites. Yet here the speaker isn't attempting to insult but commiserate, and he extends to her a kind of dignity in her lack of earthy gusto, implying that her function is to contrast with the beauty of the living world, which assumes both its full brilliance and its full sorrow only when placed beside her sadness. Far from clever cocktail talk, which is the sort of discourse Moore's poem imitates, this is the musing of a speaker whose commitment is divided between the urge to make metaphor—to be a conventional poet—and the urge to console in direct and bald exclamations. Art and society compete for his emotional commitment. The very shape of the poem, which proceeds from a concrete representation of the restaurant's sign,

L EE'S
UNCH

Spaghetti   Oysters
a Specialty   Clams

a speech-defying iconography, to the abstract exclamation of the closing lines,

What beauty
beside your sadness—and
what sorrow

embodies the development and outcome of the speaker's argument with his own aesthetic (1986, 269).

"Brilliant Sad Sun" refuses to grant a privilege to the mental state of the speaker and instead snatches at the available peaks of dramatic expression. By opening with an imitation of a sign on a restaurant rather than the human voice, the poem both problematizes the act of writing and calls attention to the analogous, radical incompletion of the speaker's argument. It also mocks, with its elliptical yet utile artifice, the cosmetically and intellectually heightened voice that in poetry usually substitutes for the voices of social discourse. Williams could imitate the meditative voice to perfection, as he does in "The Widow's Lament in Springtime," one of his best interior monologues. But here he resists the meditative mode, and in "Brilliant Sad Sun" renders only the merest outline, the rawest associations, and withholds or conceals the speaker's imperative, which seems to derive from the "sexual approach to life" that according to Mike

Weaver underlies the "sense of women and locality" in Williams's poetry (37).

Beginning with a fragment of found language, carefully framed to articulate the fragmentary overall movement of the poem, "Brilliant Sad Sun" leaps stanza by stanza to a conclusion for which the poem makes no preparation. But as I've already asserted, this conclusion is the proper closure of the speaker's argument with his own aesthetic rather than with the ostensible subject of the poem. The rhetorical structure, then, resembles the rhetorical structure of the sign in the restaurant window. This radical presentation links the dramatic association of conversation to the telegraphic communication of the restaurant sign; it omits the conventional delineation of context we expect in a novel or even a play, as well as the links that usually render the freer association of lyric intelligible.

Equally complex but differing from these procedures, Moore's "He Wrote the History Book" relies on a mock-exclamatory rhetoric of irony and whimsy together, a tonal play sufficiently dazzling to obscure the overt content and to suggest that the speaker is concealing both from the addressed person and from the reader the real emotional imperative of the poem, which is delight at the child's ability to deflate the heavy profundity of his father's great history (*the* book) and illuminate it with his whimsy. This emotional imperative, the poem's generating force, derives from the speaker's awareness of the gulf between the child's natural whimsy and her own adult commitment to intellectual ambition and accomplishment, a gulf perhaps comparable to that between the child's unconscious love of nature and the poet's "philosophical mind" explored by Wordsworth in "Ode: On Intimations of Immortality." The relationship between these minds in Moore's poem, though, is more openly dialogic:

> There! you shed a ray
>   of whimsicality on a mask of profundity so
>   terrific, that I have been dumbfounded by
> it oftener than I care to say.
>   *The* book? Titles are chaff.
>
>   Authentically
>   brief and full of energy, you contribute to your
>   father's

>   legibility and are sufficiently
>   synthetic. Thank you for showing me
>   your father's autograph. (1924, 34)

The variety of tones, from ironic to congratulatory, the deliberately exaggerated rhetorical strategies (the opening exclamation, the italicized
article in the rhetorical question), and the aggressively Latinate vocabulary ("legibility," "sufficiently," and "profundity") contrast with the simple
and anticlimactic thank-you of the closure. Unconcerned with tonal unity,
Moore here attempts to replicate the three-dimensional nuances of conversation, the psychological ambiguities that disguise themselves in the
most exact of vocabularies. She is deconstructing her own thank-you by
expressing her delight at the child's simplicity in a language of mock
profundity, and in doing so mocks herself for her Latinate expression.
The last sentence was all that was essential; but the problem of getting to
that sentence through the ponderous vocabulary is the action of the poem.

In Williams's "Complaint" the shifts in register of diction are mock
and exhausted, but lead to a glimpse of the genuine. They embody the
doctor's inability to respond to his patient as he knows he should. The
exclamation "Joy! Joy!" at the moment of delivery bitterly registers the
doctor's inability to share his patient's satisfaction (if she feels any) in suc-
cessfully giving birth; but he manages to summon a quieter, more considered and sincere compassion based on empathy by recalling his own
pleasure in the kind of act of love that results in the state this woman finds
herself. The poem opens in a tone of low-key objectivity, naturalistic and
imagistic:

>   They call me and I go.
>   It is a frozen road
>   past midnight, a dust
>   of snow caught
>   in the rigid wheeltracks.
>   The door opens.
>   I smile, enter and
>   shake off the cold (1986, 153)

But the doctor cannot shed his naturalism and objectivity when it becomes appropriate to do so. Thus he enters his patient's world with the same cold voice with which he described the natural world, which is inimical to the process occurring in the house:

> Here is a great woman
> on her side in the bed.
> She is sick,
> perhaps vomiting,
> perhaps laboring
> to give birth to
> a tenth child. Joy! Joy!

The repetition of "perhaps" betrays the doctor's uncertainty, his inability to focus; but as it occurs to him that the woman is giving birth he feels compelled to shift his register of diction and express something appropriately celebratory; hence the sarcastic interjection, the afflatus of which, in this unprepared context, is more chilling than the picture of the "frozen road" with its "snow caught / in the rigid wheeltracks." However, the registers shift again, and the doctor becomes contemplative:

> Night is a room
> darkened for lovers,
> through the jalousies the sun
> has sent one gold needle!

Here precision, instead of distancing the doctor and numbing his emotions as it did earlier in the poem, opens him to genuine empathy. The shift in tone precipitates a further shift, one in which the doctor can become almost sentimental but is saved from that lesser emotion by the way this poem has quietly earned the empathic voice, neither assuming it nor refusing it when the doctor's state of mind opens to it: "I pick the hair from her eyes / and watch her misery / with compassion." Indeed, far from sentimentalizing childbirth, the poem's closure dwells on what is most immediate, most real—its pain, sheer physical drudgery, and strain— which the doctor can readily detect but cannot understand except through this empathy.

In this brief poem the shifts in tone and registers of diction repre-

sent the contemplative processes through which the doctor attains a knowledge ordinarily forbidden to the male, even to those like Williams who
believe in the imagination. Though that knowledge is surely incomplete
and momentary, he achieves it despite the baleful influence of the frozen,
indifferent midnight snow world (which seems to reflect the doctor's
weary mood), despite exhaustion, and despite his maleness, which no
rhetoric but only the simplest observation can overcome.

My concluding example from Moore is "Black Earth," a poem whose
prosopopoeic voice interrogates itself to discover its own thematic center,
but whose topic—the power and limitations of self-expression—because
voiced by so improbable a speaker is also its central trope. The argument
of the poem is the elephant-speaker's attempt to face the problem of
power—"What is powerful and what is not?"—and his discovery that
"feats of strength [are] inexplicable after / all." He discovers not only the
"history of power" in his "back" but the limitations of speech, which are
necessarily the limitations of power, of the ego, selfhood, and history. In
recognizing in his own prosopopoeic voice the "power" to question, he
prescribes the limits of the answer in terms of simple grammatical necessity:

> The I of each is to
> the I of each,
> a kind of fretful speech
> which sets a limit on itself; the elephant is?
> (1924, 46–47)

The elephant, granted the miracle of speech by the poet, almost immediately discovers his limitations because they coincide with those of physical strength, about which he already knows a great deal. The Latinate
vocabulary of this poem is entirely unlike anything Williams would write,
but the elephant's quickly assumed empathy for the human act of speech,
derived from his ability to reason to his limits and see those as bound to
the limits of grammatical construction, is an empathy as intimately linked
to the poem's principle rhetorical strategies as the more conventionally
human empathy the doctor discovers in "Complaint."

When the elephant, considering the totality of himself, his trunk,
his self-questioning, is moved to conclude his poem he does so with
another question:

                    Will
depth be depth, thick skin be thick, to one who can see
                    no
beautiful element of unreason under it?

The world "described by [his] trunk" has expanded with every question;
and now, in the closure, the final question is freighted with both the
precisely delineated fleshiness of the beast and the ability to abstract, to
reason or unreason, to allegorize, if need be. The elephant cannot solve
either the puzzle of his body or the puzzle of reason, but he can in the
end formulate the proper question. Freely exercising the interrogative
mode leads him to externalize the trope of prosopopoeia and characterize its limits by the similes he applies to his physical state of being:

        This elephant skin
            which I inhabit, fibred over like the shell of
        the cocoanut, this piece of black glass through
                            which   no light

    can filter—cut
    into checkers by rut
            upon rut of unpreventable experience—
            it is a manual for the peanut-tongued and the

        hairy toed.

By sampling the tentative, arbitrary modes of rhetoric he comes to understand that these qualities embody a peculiar kind of truth, and that the
ambiguous, artificial mode of speech that has given him voice can demonstrate what plain statement is too shy to embrace. To place this power
of questioning and quality of language-perception in the voice of a beast
of muscular power and enormous fleshiness and allow it to speak in such
a rotund and Latinate manner surely pushes prosopopoeia to the brink of
the pathetic fallacy. In this poem the language of flesh and the language of
ratiocination merge in a oddly colloquial and extraliterary manner as peculiar to Moore as Williams's "quick changes of tone, atmosphere, and
speed" are to him.

    Both poets devise specific rhetorical and psychological strategies in response to the problem of dispensing with the conventional range of poetic voices available to the poetry of their time. Rejecting the drive for "pure poetry" that characterized the lyric poetry of the 1890s and the first decade of the twentieth century, Williams and Moore in their use of extraliterary modes of language, argument, and persuasion inevitably fashioned antipodal poetries. The point of their refusal of settled modes of discourse was not to create yet another school of like-thinking poets but to extend the available modes of rhetoric, as Wordsworth and Coleridge did in the conversation poem. However vital their aesthetic distinctions, Moore and Williams both attained to a form of writing that would embrace a range of discourse as wide as the urban American experience they shared. This mutual faith was the source of earnest if qualified respect that usually engendered sympathetic though sometimes puzzled responses to each other's work over the course of their writing lives. Their rhetorical strategies pushed American poetry into idiomatic language, colloquial phrasing, nonmetrical rhythm, and informal syntax. Unlike Pound and Eliot, they were concerned less with the history of poetry than with its peculiarly American future.

Eliot & Pound

Political Discourse and the Voicing of Difference

The dialogic imperative of language, underscored by the modernist embrace of dramatic and narrative devices, draws attention to the inequalities of power among interlocutors. Distributing or retaining the power of discourse is a political issue because it determines the form a given community of speakers and listeners will take and defines the terms and scope of their communications. T.S. Eliot and Ezra Pound were the most politically and socially engaged poets of their generation. Unfortunately, as is well known, this engagement from the start was corrupted by ideas of social and cultural exclusivity, and eventually expressed itself as anti-Semitism and, in Pound's case, the enthusiastic embrace of fascism. However, in their earlier work their larger social concerns engender powerful senses of the political subtleties of rhetoric, and generate poetry in which the speaking voices achieve dramatic and psychological nuances comparable to those found in the novels of Henry James and James Joyce. This chapter will examine Eliot's "Portrait of a Lady" and Pound's *Hugh Selwyn Mauberley* as instances of this rhetorical subtlety and invention.

"Portrait of a Lady"

The argument of Eliot's "Portrait of a Lady" revolves around the speaker's desire to assume control of the poem's discourse and invert the power relationship between himself and the lady. To do this he requires the reader to recognize the sociocultural mystification of the lady's speech by participating in his understanding of discursive politics. Further, he expects to persuade the reader to reject the Edwardian world of the drawing room in favor of the symbolist world of the urban streets. The ways Eliot imagines and gives voice to his speaker and projects and addresses his audience suggest a great deal about how he regards individuality and community, which he recognizes as involving political and social issues as well as aesthetic ones. The problem of poetic authority, too, is a political issue, one that preoccupied Eliot early in his career, as Louis Menand, Russell Kirk, and other critics have shown. The issue, in brief, is that the authority of the poet's self-presentation derives either from individual peculiarities and eccentricities—that is, from the way a poet challenges what he or she takes to be traditional expectations—or from the manner in which the poet makes a show of reaffirming a tradition by selectively conforming to its historical dictates. More profoundly, a poem usually either challenges or affirms the ordinary discourse of its cultural milieu. Eliot's poetry is complex enough to do both. Of the great modernists, Joyce and Eliot followed Pound in clearly demanding the authority both of originality and tradition. Eliot spent a long writing life defining the terms of that composite authority.

"Portrait of a Lady" exemplifies Eliot's early strategies for inventing a voice sufficient to his complex purpose, one that works to control the discourse to favor its own point of view, yet which through the admission of dialogue and consequent dialectic concedes an indeterminate power to another—the lady in this instance—and to the reader. As Edward Said points out in discussing Joyce, "The situation of discourse . . . hardly puts equals face to face. Rather, discourse places one interlocutor above another" (48–49). It is a mark of Eliot's honesty of purpose, his sense of the poem as a place of struggle rather than of aesthetic harmony, that he often requires his speakers to struggle from the position of the less empowered interlocutor. In *The Waste Land,* for instance, the speaker cannot enter into dialogue with the nervous woman whose voice dominates "A Game of Chess." When she demands, "I never know what you are thinking. Think," she implicitly refuses him speech, and he compliantly meditates, conceding to her the empowerment of discourse: "I think we are in rats' alley / Where the dead men lost their bones."

As Said argues, the depiction of speech is crucial to a literary text attempting to claim a place in the world by calling attention to its worldliness: "In producing texts with either a firm claim on, or an explicit will to worldliness, these writers and genres have valorized speech, making it the tentacle by which an otherwise silent text ties itself into the world of discourse" (45).

Worldliness is an historical and social characteristic. V.N.Volosinov explains how reported speech becomes valorized—how it assumes historical and social dimensions—by referring to the explicitly social assumptions we make when confronted with dialogue:

> What we have in the forms of reported speech is precisely an objective document of this reception. Once we have learned to decipher it, this document provides us with information, not about accidental and mercurial subjective psychological processes in the "soul" of the recipient, but about steadfast social tendencies in an active reception of other speakers' speech, tendencies that have crystallized into language forms. (117)

Since society seems a more authentic concept than the soul (one believes or disbelieves in the soul, while automatically conceding existence to society), so speech claims an illusion of actuality unavailable to the interior monologue—though of course a philosophical idealist would offer another view. Eliot's early poems are resolutely social. By accepting the silence of meditation, the speaker of *The Waste Land* accepts a less privileged role in the larger world of discourse. To gain a position of greater empowerment is the task that the speaker of "Portrait of a Lady" sets for himself. Examining his approach to the problem will, I hope, shed some light on the essentially political purpose of Eliot's appropriation of the techniques of prose fiction as well as his incorporation of Laforgue's rhetoric of irony and the language of the urban streets.

In *The Egoist* of September 1918, in the first of four articles entitled "Reflections on Contemporary Poetry," Eliot argued that "one of the ways by which contemporary verse has tried to escape the rhetorical, the abstract, the moralizing, to recover (for that is its purpose) the accents of direct speech, is to concentrate its attention upon trivial or accidental or commonplace objects" (1917, 4.8:118). The key phrase here is the "*accents* of direct speech": poetry need not, should not attempt to reproduce speech in its garrulity and commonness, but by catching something of its tone and ambiguity can appropriate the worldliness and dramatic power of actual discourse.

Eliot certainly sensed that he was about to reissue Wordsworth's call for speech purification, since he then turned the essay into a discussion of the sources of emotion in poetry, using Wordsworth not as an example of a poet using speech-accents but one whose emotions are "vague," though at least backed by philosophy. However, what causes more concern here is the rest of Eliot's opening passage. The misleading words are "trivial," "accidental," and "commonplace." The verse of the French poets of the late nineteenth century and the verse of Donne and some of the other seventeenth-century English poets illuminate, not merely reproduce, the trivial, and this power of illumination is exactly what Eliot admired in his favorite lyric and meditative poets, not merely their subject matter—which, as he notes in other essays, is the common property of the avant-garde. But the power of illumination is essentially proprietary, something Eliot attempts to reserve for himself and to share, through the displacement of opposing interlocutor, with his fictional speaker.

The article goes on to discuss the ways in which poets of various cultures use the trivial. Americans rest everything on the accidental object—a generalization to which William Carlos Williams probably would have been happy to accede. British poets merely become preoccupied with trivia, according it no special emotional endowment. Although Eliot claims that "in his difference the American shows his too quick susceptibility to foreign influences," he is clearly American himself in this regard, as well as in his embrace of the accidental trivia of urban life. Even the earliest poems in the Berg Collection reveal a preoccupation with the potential of the trivia for bearing emotional weight. In one poem entitled "First Caprice in North Cambridge," dating from about 1909, broken glass and mud and the music of a tinny piano (which Piers Gray claims in Laforgue's "Autre Complainte de Lord Pierrot" is a "symbolic expression of the inner self" [10]) constitute the aesthetic of visual and aural expression that Eliot would later oppose to the muted and corrupt sensuality of the Edwardian world of his middle-class youth. Another, dated 1910, on the subject of Easter, revolves around potted plants and the odor of heat in city streets. In these apprentice poems the images have not yet attained the emotional luminescence such trivia display in "Portrait of a Lady," but they direct the reader to an aesthetic anti-ideal, their presence arguing that the source of art is in the commonplace.

Symbolist tactics attempt to decenter the speaker by placing him in an unwholesome, primitive, but inspirational environment, and therefore deflect the elitism of the romantic author's expressionist claims to privileged insight. But symbolism makes an equally extravagant claim, not about the author but about subject matter and style, about the relationship between sign and referent, idealizing not the perception of the speaker but what he perceives. That the symbolist imagery speaks, as Louis Menand has pointed out, "to others" (18), not the poet-speaker, is significant, but not as important as the way the poet assumes an authoritative, even authoritarian, point of view. The poet's manipulation of images not for their sensuous qualities but for their emotional and political purposes, to empower certain aspects of their discourse at the expense of other modes, is the central strategy of poems like "Portrait of a Lady."

In his discussion of the use of "trivial" and usually urban subject matter, Eliot does not explicitly describe the political significance of the stance the speaker of the poem assumes toward both the subject matter and the audience (both the fictional audience within the poem—the lady, who at times assumes the role of audience and at other times the role of speaker—and the actual audience without). In "Portrait of a Lady" the strategy of the speaker is to ask the reader to weigh one mode of discourse against another, to weigh the Edwardian cultured seductions of the lady against the young man's symbolist embrace of the commonplace. Presumably, the reader will comply in empowering the discourse of the street. The drawing room discourse offers no advantage except that the author presents it as speech. Whether this socially advantageous positioning of the lady as interlocutor outweighs the disadvantages of her role constitutes part of the dilemma the poem attempts to resolve.

In the words of Ludmilla Gruszewska-Wojtas, "in the drawing-room art does not constitute any creative potential but simply one more static, decorative element which suits the general image of the upper class world" (74). If the reader judged merely on the abstract consideration of aesthetic viability, the symbolism of the street world would displace the static world of the drawing room, but other factors enter the poem. One is the character of the speaker, who is timid, self-deluding, and insincere. The character of the lady is more developed; her speech, presented as dialogue, is idealized by her dramatic, novelistic presentation; and her nostalgia, however sentimental, seems more mature and heartfelt than the young man's callow and shamefaced refusal of her. In weighing speech against meditation, moreover, extralinguistic factors enter. The reader may feel that in a poem, and possibly as well in a novel, more "truth" may reside in the meditative voice, which makes us privy to what purport to be private thoughts with no social need for dissemblance. The public utterance implies an immediate presence, a direct imitation of discourse. But in the relatively intimate utterance of the brief poem, such presence cannot dominate the situation the way it might in a novel, with its fuller, more inclusive representation of the actual world of discourse.

The poem, then, functions as a complex of rhetorical strategies and stances, all of which serve to further delineate and differentiate the fictional construct of the speaker and the two other participants, one intra-poem and one externalized, the first as fictional as the speaker, the other not fictional at all. The triangular relationship is definitive; if the author-speaker weren't also a fictional construct but only the intratextual participant, the lady herself would be fictional and would unassailably dominate the poem's world of discourse. The privilege of art would hinge entirely on her dialogue, and the speaker's psychological self-musings would too freely distinguish themselves from the dramatic-emotional situation, which the poem constructs by imitating conversation not meditation. In other words, the poem would consist of her dialogue, and the speaker would assume the extratextual role of critic.

Therefore if we were to read this poem as autobiography we could not accept its fiction of the completely enclosed triangulated world, and the author-speaker would be unable to appropriate the powerful discourse of the culturally and dramatically privileged lady. Thus bracketed from the actual world of discourse, yet worldly in its acknowledgment of the power and necessity of speech, the poem is free to mediate between two modes of presentation: the imitation of speech and the imitation of thought and meditation. Through temporal engagement the poem temporarily fictionalizes the reader so that the illusion of dramatic enclosure becomes complete, the reader's complicity assured. Though this is a valuable strategy in satire, it is alien to the autobiographical poem, since the world of autobiography is of necessity a solitary one. The self-musing of the autobiographer is common to lyric but distinct from the voice or voices of dramatic, novelistic poems. When Eliot wrote the occasional obviously autobiographical poem, usually marked by lyric discontinuity, he was likely to leave it unpublished, or, as in the case of "Ode," originally printed in *Ara Vos Prec* (1920), to exclude it from later publications. Most of Eliot's published early poems (before *Ash Wednesday*), despite their psychological obsessions, choose their strategies of voice and rhetoric to help avoid characteristically autobiographical expression. Perhaps incidentally, but certainly with the firmness of realist fiction, these strategies establish a community of speaker and reader that often implicates the latter in acts of class definition and unconscious exclusion. Even without our participatory awareness these poems, like the novel of Henry James from which Eliot derived his title, stroke our egos by offering us roles of superior psychological and social insight and satiric conspiracy.

The dialogue of "Portrait of a Lady," then, both encourages us to understand the poem as a fiction, an act of containment, and to understand its bonds with the familiar social world of discourse. To step out of the three-person community (lady, speaker, reader) would betray it by exposing it as a construct, which Eliot does only to reengage it with greater tenacity. Betraying the community of three undermines the whole idea of community, which requires the temporary containment of opposing forces. Cuckoldry and seduction clearly signal that these forces cannot be contained for long, which is why these acts are too serious to discuss other than humorously. The lady of this portrait invites betrayal because preparing her room with "An atmosphere of Juliet's tomb," as the speaker morbidly sees it, she tries too hard to exclude the "false note" that would shatter, however momentarily, the world of the drawing room. Therefore, in every way she invites precisely that shattering, which happens when the speaker betrays her to the reader through manipulations of rhetoric, memory, and the first-person plural pronoun.

The speaker cannot express to her his sense of change, the pressure of her aesthetic of life-as-rhetoric which so depresses him that her voice "returns like the insistent out-of-tune / Of a broken violin on an August afternoon." The dialogue consists of two discourse-situations—the lady to the speaker, the speaker to the reader—and the irony of the poem lies in the use of the pronoun "we," which sometimes means lady and speaker, sometimes speaker and reader. Thus the community of the poem is based on irony, which is the opposition of feeling to expression, and the betrayal of the lady is necessary as the poem sacrifices her confidences for the greater confidence with which it addresses the reader.

The poem is in three parts, the first a recollection of a gray Decem-

ber afternoon, the second a still-funereal April dusk, and the third an
October evening; so the impression is of a single afternoon and evening
that nevertheless spans most of a year. The first section depicts a decidedly Jamesian encounter in which the speaker addresses the lady as if she
were present and not the fictional reconstruction from memory suggested
by the selection and patterning of imagery:

> Among the smoke and fog of a December afternoon
> You have the scene arrange itself—as it will seem to do—
> With "I have saved this afternoon for you";
> And four wax candles in the darkened room,
> Four rings of light upon the ceiling overhead,
> An atmosphere of Juliet's tomb
> Prepared for all the things to be said, or left unsaid.

The atmosphere in the room is literary, nineteenth century, and "traditional" in the popular usage of the term, a usage Eliot explicitly rejected
in "Tradition and the Individual Talent" (1919). Such an idea of tradition
is not only metaphysically numbing but bears too heavy an investment in
the language of death, the very language that in the closure of the poem
returns in a more "modern," more "trivial," "accidental," and more significant because emotionally supercharged vocabulary. The image of "four
wax candles in the darkened room" is replaced by the more Laforgue-like
"afternoon grey and smoky, evening yellow and rose," and the speaker
offers no obvious literary allusions, lays no claim upon tradition.

But in the opening section, as the speaker recalls the lady as she was
in December, literature, tradition, and high culture are much on his mind.
That they function here as the trappings of the bourgeoisie is intimated
by the painstaking artificiality of the lady's speech:

> "So intimate, this Chopin, that I think his soul
> Should be resurrected only among friends
> Some two or three, who will not touch the bloom
> That is rubbed and questioned in the concert room."

Eliot's distaste for the middle class later finds expression in an article
in *The Criterion,* entitled "In Memoriam: Marie Lloyd," in which he not

only mourns the death of the famous music-hall performer but the failure of the middle class (British, in this instance) to find a proper means of cultural expression. The lower classes at least have the music halls, but with their "decay . . . with the encroachment of the cheap and rapidly breeding cinema, the lower classes will tend to drop into the same state of protoplasm as the bourgeoisie" (1951, 458). Eliot thought this essay significant enough, despite the nonliterary subject, to include it in *Selected Essays.*

For Eliot, as for Baudelaire and Laforgue, the language of the city is one of the stays against the collapse into "protoplasm." Evoking this language (which is hardly peculiar to Eliot but assumes fresh authority in these poems) enables the speaker to situate himself in relation to both the lady and the auditor-reader. "Smoke and fog," in an era when cities burned coal, a "tobacco trance," "books," "public clocks," "street piano," or "comics and sporting page," while not insistently urban, are so nonaesthetic and so clearly not of the vocabulary of nature that, like references to skyscrapers or the Brooklyn Bridge, they constitute a distinctly urban language. As everyone knows, Eliot learned to use this language from Baudelaire and Laforgue. But clearly the vocabulary, the voice, and the stance confirmed an affinity already present in his sensibility. The previously cited *Egoist* article, as if anticipating Harold Bloom's theory of poetic influence, describes the process by which a writer absorbs the very soul, as it were, of a predecessor:

> This relation is a feeling of profound kinship, or
> rather of a peculiar personal intimacy, with another,
> probably a dead author. It may overcome us sud-
> denly, on first or after long acquaintance; it is cer-
> tainly a crisis; and when a young writer is seized
> with his first passion of this sort he may be changed,
> metamorphosed almost, within a few weeks, from
> a bundle of secondhand sentiments into a person.
> (1917, 4.10:151)

That this statement should appear in a journal entitled *The Egoist* is a happy coincidence, since no clearly more concise explanation of the formation of a *writer's* ego exists. The point here is that Eliot did not merely imitate Laforgue; he absorbed him because Eliot was already prepared by temperament, inclination, and the reading of Baudelaire for a new language that would enable him to render with proper irony his young man's delicate sense of the ridiculous and his Baudelairean and Dantean vision of the metropolis as inferno.

To return to the poem: in the opening verse paragraph the speaker offers asides to the reader: "We have been, let us say . . . / —And so the conversation slips"; while in the second verse paragraph, the final twelve lines of part 1, he drops the pretense of listening to the lady and focuses, for the benefit of the reader, on his own psychological process, which is "hammering a prelude of its own," introducing the "false note" the lady of this portrait has apparently dedicated her life to excluding. The memory of the "dull tom-tom" in his brain is the rhythmic adolescent (and proto-symbolist) carpe diem, the insistence on escaping stifling conformity and getting on with one's life. But the we to whom this message refers are not the speaker and the lady but the speaker and the reader, that nonfictional auditor who is the real confidant of the poem.

Some commentators have discussed "Portrait of a Lady" as a "descriptive monologue" in which "the lady is at once pitiful and odd; the young man inept and supercilious " (Smith, 9–10); as a James short story dealing in "muted desperation and polite betrayal" (Bergonzi, 12); and as a psychodrama of victimizing and victimization (Pinion, 73). I have no quarrel with these or other readings of the poem: I only want to call attention to the speaker's deliberate, calculated manipulation of subject and audience, and especially to the fact that the speaker engages the reader in a conspiracy against the lady. This is a novelistic strategy Eliot learned from Conrad, a manipulation of voice that as A. Walton Litz has pointed out has a great deal to do with Eliot's later shaping of The Waste Land (18).

To argue that this is a political act is not to say it is not literary as well but to assert that literary and social concerns meet when literature invokes the actual world of discourse to claim for itself that illusion of presence Said calls "worldliness." The act of the speaker is political because it deliberately subverts the lady's attempt to include him in her perception of community and because the young man implicitly rejects her since she is embarrassingly bourgeois and her aestheticism is inadequate to even her own emotional needs. In addition, her willingness to expose her emotional difficulties, even in dispassionate and defeated language, threatens the young man's self-possession, a thin disguise for what Richard Shusterman calls his "callow, self-protecting selfishness and fear of candor" (98). His emotional life is no more enriched by his ironic, symbolist aesthetic than hers is by her Edwardian formalism, but politically hers is the more suspect position, since she embodies the cultural pretensions of the middle class Eliot found so distasteful.

Of course, Eliot is no Marxist but rather a young man attempting to formulate a vision of culture, neither conservative nor radical, that despite or perhaps because of his ten years' study of philosophy he needs in order to adequately distinguish literature from metaphysics. This vision, like "Tradition and the Individual Talent," would "halt at the frontiers of metaphysics or mysticism" (1951, 21). Eliot intended to be practical in his criticism and disparaged his tendency toward abstract thinking, but to become politically conscious as a critic is to theorize. He claims in a late essay, published as *The Frontiers of Criticism,* that his best work is "essays on poets and poetic dramatists who had influenced him" (1956, 7). Late as these comments come, they are consistent with Eliot's outlook and practice throughout his poetic career—though his career as social critic is another matter.

The point is that whatever looks like social or aesthetic criticism in "Portrait of a Lady" is not programmatic or theoretically formulated but pragmatically conceived. The poem is about its own point of view, about the manipulation of that point of view, about the attempt to transcend that dreadful burden we call the self, which in lyric or meditative poetry (though not necessarily in dramatic or narrative poetry) manifests its presence most directly through the exposition of an interior point of view. James Longenbach points out that "Portrait" is among those poems Eliot characterized in the 1926 Clark lectures as "'phenomenological poems,' poems spoken by personae who fall into the trap of interpretation" (1987, 184). But I'm not sure that "trap" is the best word. The speaker of "Portrait" may be entrapped, but his strategy is to enlarge the boundaries of his confinement by drawing the reader into the act of interpretation, thus preventing the potentially closed world of the poem—bourgeois, stifling, aphoristic, and genteel as it is—from entirely cocooning him.

Having violated the decorum at the end of part 1 of this tripartite world by confiding to the reader his psychological unease, the speaker returns in the April dusk to report the further confidences (contrived as they are) of this lady of uncertain age. At first she seems to reprove him, perhaps for revealing her confidences to us: "Ah my friend, you do not know, you do not know / What life is, you who hold it in your hands." But although she wants to suggest he holds some power over her, it is actually his life of which she speaks, not her own. In fact, he has no power over her, not even to betray her, since the surface she presents is so complete, so finished, that it cannot be violated.

What can be violated is the pretense that this is a confidential situation, and the speaker turns to us with "of course" to alert us to the irony with which he views both the colloquy and his very presence:

> "You let it flow from you [life], you let it flow,
> And youth is cruel, and has no remorse
> And smiles at situations which it cannot see."
> I smile, of course,
> And go on drinking tea.

Who is holding whose life in hand? He acknowledges her mild criticism in a predictable way, exposing himself to her as exactly the callow young man she expects him to be, while exposing himself to us as a Laforguean ironist in the making. The two-faced quality of this smile means nothing to her, only to the reader, and in this further betrayal our complicity is assured.

The speaker no longer hesitates to assure us of his distaste for the lady's conversation, and by describing her voice as a broken violin (mocking her cultural pretensions) he primes us with irony for her words to follow, which are out of tune with her feelings much as the street piano is out of tune with Chopin's musical aspirations:

> "I am always sure that you understand
> My feelings, always sure that you feel,
> Sure that across the gulf you reach your hand."

Yet the reader may feel a pang here. Surely she understands the irony of her comment, if not the irony with which it is received? But by voicing the fact of her feelings, however distorted by mannerism, she exerts control over the emotional tone of the poem at a key moment, one in which the sympathy of the reader is likely to be swayed her way. One weakness of the symbolist approach is its refusal of the direct voice of emotion, or so the poem here seems to suggest; yet the world of the drawing room restricts emotional expression at least as severely as the world of the street does. That her voice is "out-of-tune" not only mocks her but reminds the reader that emotions cannot be precisely voiced; yet her willingness to bring up the subject of emotions enables her to retain, for a moment, the upper hand and prevent the poem from concluding with the symbolist street scene, the irony of which would almost wholly negate her pathos. That pathos also is ironic, and perhaps even foolish, but it is human.

By insisting on the lady's "velleities and carefully caught regrets" the speaker attempts to prevent the reader from hearing her as the dominant consciousness of the poem; his screening and selection of her monologue fictionalizes her as an insipid, pretentious bore, yet his fascination with her, though largely elided, remains a necessary guiding hypothesis. Now, in fact, the speaker begins to regret his ready irony, his attempt to betray her to the reader, and, stung by her rebuke, he departs to immerse himself in the emotionally neutral language of public discourse:

> I take my hat: how can I make a cowardly amends
> For what she has said to me?
> You will see me any morning in the park
> Reading the comics and the sporting page.

However, this respite through immersion in ordinary, nonemotionally charged discourse cannot last, since his meditative voice isn't dramatic enough to sustain the poem without the counterpoint of her speech. The speaker confesses that even his symbolist street world reminds him of her emotional imperatives, partly because, despite its vulgar immediacy, it shares the emotional and artistic inadequacies of her Edwardian aestheticism:

> I remain self-possessed
> Except when a street-piano, mechanical and tired
> Reiterates some worn-out common song
> With the smell of hyacinths across the garden

Recalling things that other people have desired.
Are these ideas right or wrong?

This last appeal to the reader is a deceptive or two-faced plea. What "ideas" does he mean? Does this Bradleyan young man think he can link his symbolist insights to emotional imperatives derived from "things that other people have desired"? (Of which sorts of desires does this young man want us to approve?) His problem is that he cannot openly speak for himself, as the lady does, but has imprisoned himself in a world of symbols. These, despite their material insistence, yield little more than a nostalgic presence and an embodiment of his ironic but self-defeating or self-deluding stance. Although the symbolist aesthetic is directly opposed to her variety of aestheticism, it is inadequate, in part, because it too readily embraces cultural primitivism. As Shusterman argues,

> Eliot seems to be suggesting here that though art must not altogether abandon its more primitive roots, rhythms, and life energies, a full return to primitivism is not a viable solution for Western aesthetics. Though we may despise sophisticated decadence, we cannot be fully satisfied by naive primitivism which is ultimately false to our experience and thus, for us, involves a sophisticated posturing and escapism of its own. (107)

The slackest moments of the drama occur on an October night that "comes down" with the heaviness of an old cliché. The speaker returns to the lady's rooms "as before / Except for a slight sensation of being ill at ease." In fact, this sensation is so great that when he has reached the top of the stairs he feels as though he has "mounted on [his] hands and knees." The speaker is about to embark for Europe, where presumably he will confront firsthand the culture this lady attempts to foster and embody. But he may already have lost his Jamesian innocence, a loss represented by his disembodied smile that "falls heavily among the bric-à-brac," the detritus of a trivialized high culture.

Now the lady turns to more personal matters, and the speaker for a moment regains his "self-possession," since he had expected the topic of their relationship to arise. Yet, faced with the actuality of her discrete passion for him (how else can we understand her wondering "Why we have not developed into friends"?), his malleable smile fails him and he becomes even more self-conscious than at any other moment in the poem. Even now, at the crisis, he tries to include the reader (for it is the reader who is in his confidence, not the lady), in his dismay:

> I feel like one who smiles, and turning shall remark
> Suddenly, his expression in a glass.
> My self-possession gutters; we are really in the dark.

The lady again has the advantage, so she consolidates her position by outlining for him a fuller glimpse of the little community he has violated with his ironies and appeals to nonfictional auditors:

> "For everybody said so, all our friends,
> They were all sure our feelings would relate
> So closely! I myself can hardly understand.
> We must leave it now to fate.
> You will write, at any rate.
> Perhaps it is not too late.
> I shall sit here serving tea to friends."

The witty triple rhyme rings with a dismissal almost as scornful and economical as "Mistah Kurtz—he dead," Conrad's abrupt refusal of white imperialist culture. But it falls flat on her audience. The young man is not merely insensitive; he clearly sees her feelings and consciously, guiltily rejects them, partly because he's offended by the language in which she presents herself, and partly because he's afraid of both her and his own feelings.

While the lady continues her settled routine of serving tea and platonically or perhaps actually seducing young men, the speaker must embrace the larger urban world to find the symbolism that may or may not sustain him, engaging the reader, his one firm link with the world beyond the poem, in a quest for significant form:

> And I must borrow every changing shape
> To find expression . . . dance, dance
> Like a dancing bear,

Cry like a parrot, chatter like an ape.
Let us take the air, in a tobacco trance—

But now that the lady has dismissed him, much as he has long since dismissed her attempts at intimacy, he wonders what would happen to his little world if she died and left him "sitting pen in hand / With the smoke coming down about the housetops." Without her, he wouldn't know "what to feel," since her presence and her speech-valorized voice trigger that self-sustaining irony beyond which he has no emotional life. How is he to regard himself? Wise, foolish, tardy, "too soon"? The reader can't help him. But what makes "This music . . . successful" is that with his fall from her grace and the turning inward of his voice he can face a real issue, "talk of dying," and explicitly ask whether he has the "right to smile." At last he deliberately rather than unconsciously turns his irony on himself. If he remains a satirist of a single note he has grown into a more marked self-awareness, and like all good Jamesian heroes he has gained a small degree of psychological freedom, though at great emotional cost. More significantly for my argument, he has done this by stepping outside of the usual boundaries of narrative, has invoked the reader for a variety of rhetorical purposes, and has asked the auditor to bear witness, as no one in the poem can, to the struggle to escape the various multidimensional but self-limited fictional communities he creates—that of the seductive lady and reluctant young man, that of her larger circle of acquaintance, that of speaker and reader, and that larger world enclosed by the poem, a world made possible by imposing lyric closure on a poem that is both monologic and dialogic. Though, as Stanley Sultan says, this poem, like *The Waste Land,* ends with "the protagonist's destiny not portrayed: the action developed to its resolution but his story not concluded," it is a poem not of action so much as the refusal to act, and of choosing a lyrical stance, circular though it is, to assert his independence from a situation he cannot resolve (180).

Eliot's regard for the shifting narrative stances of Conrad, the psychological characterization of James, and the symbol-laden irony of Laforgue does not by any means constitute his entire aesthetic. But the politics of discourse in which the speakers of his poems through *The Waste Land* engage, exposing their attitudes toward and manipulation of social and cultural communities, derive in part from his receptivity to these sources. "Portrait of a Lady" is called Laforgean, and indeed it is, but its narration is more complex and novelistic than anything in the French poet's lyric meditations.

Armed with this reading, we could examine other poems including "Prufrock" and *The Waste Land* and discover how they too use speakers who resist the author's need to impose the larger world of discourse on his poems and thereby expose the psychological forces, the unkempt will and desire, the fears and self-recriminations that empower his complex poetics. Driven by half-repressed emotions, these speakers shift their stance to violate the conventions of their self-contained world. They violate the confidences of fictional bourgeois communities by exposing their conflicting internal forces, and they expand the possibilities of poetry by appealing to the reader to break down the wall, at least momentarily, between the fiction of the speaker and the actuality of the audience. Clearly *The Waste Land,* with its single consciousness and multiple speakers, its manipulation of pronominal voices (from "we" to "you" to "I" in "The Burial of the Dead," for example, and the return to the second-person plural in "What the Thunder Said," only to abandon it at the poem's climax) invites this sort of reading, but would require a much longer exposition than this one devoted to "Portrait."

In the ongoing reconsideration of Eliot, a process of revisionary reading afforded only the most compelling of poets, it is worthwhile to consider again Pound's dictum that poetry be at least as well written as prose, consider that for both Pound and Eliot this dictum referred not merely to grammar, texture, and syntax but also to large strategies, to the invention and manipulation of dramatic voices, to psychological characterization and narrative devices, and to awareness of the political nature of discourse and dialectic. They learned these not from French symbolism or from troubadour poets but from the masters of English and French prose—Henry James, Gustave Flaubert, Joseph Conrad, James Joyce, and perhaps even Ford Madox Ford.

The use of narrative devices and the opposition of meditative and speaking voices to refute the fiction of a homogeneous social and aesthetic community is a common project in modern literature. If I have failed to demonstrate this in regard to "Portrait of a Lady," the argument may seem more convincing if I refer the reader to Conrad's *Heart of Darkness* and the little community of five upon whom Marlowe makes such demands with his tale; or to Henry James's *The Aspern Papers* in which the speaker violates forever a fragile community of two founded on memory, loss, and emotional instability; or to *Ulysses,* the most political of novels in the most political (that is, socially aware and power conscious) of voices, one that does not hesitate to make the most absurd and engaging appeals to the reader.

After Eliot's equally demanding use of self-reflexive narrative devices in *The Waste Land,* the manipulative use of voice would no longer be central to his poems. The quieter meditative poems following "The Hollow Men" do not politicize their voices the way "Portrait of a Lady" does, do not by means of appeal to the reader use the ethos of fiction to oppose one interlocutor to another in order to illustrate the indeterminate nature of art and culture. Instead, the voices of *Ash Wednesday* and *Burnt Norton* reject the random worldliness of discourse in favor of a more hermetic world where nostalgia for revelation and epiphany supplement the unappeasable desire for community. But in his earlier poems Eliot extends in many ways the available range of dramatic and interior voices, and only occasionally have the poets after him demonstrated comparable mastery of these rhetorical strategies, or a similar understanding of the social and psychological complexities that give them significance.

Hugh Selwyn Mauberley

Like Eliot, Ezra Pound invokes and problematizes ideas of community by manipulating dialogic voices and testing the limits of restricting genres. *Hugh Selwyn Mauberley* comments upon the revisionary aesthetic of English poets in the 1890s who resisted Browning and the dramatic monologue by attempting to reinvent a "pure poetry" of unalloyed lyric and thus liberate emotional expression from the particulars of historical context. Of course, once history had reentered verse, once Browning had demonstrated the power and vitality of the new genre, there was no turning back. Pound's own aesthetic, derived from (among other sources) both Browning and the poets of the 1890s, as demonstrated in *Mauberley,* retains Browning's grip on history but turns the dramatic monologue around. Instead of writing a narrative monologue infused with lyric moments, Pound writes a sequence of lyrics knitted together with a single monologic voice interrupted by the brief dramatic interjections of other characters.

Much of the critical confusion surrounding *Mauberley* derives from attempts to divide the poem into two distinct voices, one referred to as Pound the other as Mauberley, each commenting on the other as artistic Quixote of an age of grimaces and broken statuary. This results in canards such as the claim that "Medallion" is a deliberately weak poem designed to embody Mauberley's shortcomings, or the reverse, that "Envoi" sums up the weakness of Pound's early poetry and embodies the failure of *Mauberley* itself. Pound would have disdained such expressive fallacies, but some of his critics have embraced them. Others, more plausibly, have argued that the voice of the poem is singular, a persona of the poet that modulates radically as it tests various stances, various aspects of the problem of the artist's divided consciousness in a hostile and destructive era.

This singular voice, however, like that of Tiresias in *The Waste Land,* is one of witness and criticism, not of dramatic participation. But unlike Tiresias, it repeatedly talks itself into lyric closure; thus in formal terms as well as psychological ones it resists participation in the narrative continuity of the larger story the poem recounts. This voice is psychologically distinct from Pound speaking for himself and strategically different from the development of Mauberley as a central character distinct from Pound. Mauberley is not exactly the "untrustworthy critic" Jo Berryman describes (1); rather he is an imitation of the role of untrustworthy critic as Pound would play it, if the poem were about Pound rather than Mauberley. The first poem in the sequence, Pound's self-eulogy, ranges over most of the available registers of diction and voice, and constitutes a guide to and precis of all that follows. The two sections of the sequence portray various available aesthetic or poetic personae available to the central consciousness and mimetic voice. In "E.P." this consciousness is active enough to speak its own elegy and to eulogize its less aesthetically vital aspect as "Mauberley," a persona (in Pound's primary sense, a mask) unable to speak for himself. This proprietary voice is a uniting consciousness that "sees all" in somewhat the way that Tiresias "sees all" to hold *The Waste Land* together. The difference, though, is essential: Pound maintains a dramatic distance by retaining the privilege of lyric closure, and does not limit this persona to dramatically identifiable characteristics. He is either a first person or a third person presence, and we cannot even say with confidence that the first person pronominal voice narrates the "Mauberley" section or "Yeux Glauques," or sections I, II, IV, V, X, and XI of part 1. Yet the consciousness is consistent, the voice singular, despite shifts in person, and the inclusive first-person plural, when it infrequently occurs, provides the essential clue to a reading of this poem.

For Pound wants "us" to understand this poem as one in which "we" have a stake. His purpose is frankly didactic, though what he is being didactic about is not entirely obvious. Certainly the destruction—glorious, in some ways, Pound can't help but notice—of civilization is an important issue; but more central to this poem (and failure to note this is one reason some critics have gone astray) is the split in aesthetic consciousness that Pound believed plagued the modern writer, a split represented by the tension between lyric and monologue and by the division of the sequence into two sections.

This split suggests Eliot's "dissociation of sensibility," which though presented by him as a literary-historical issue is actually a fiction, like all such dualisms, an imaginary systemization of complexities otherwise too muddy to function in the allegorical pressures of the poem (Eliot's criticism, like Pound's, is an extension of his poetry, not an independent enterprise). It is useless, though, to denigrate Eliot's and Pound's penchant for dualism. The arbitrary ordering such fictions facilitate helped shape their art, most obviously in poems like *The Waste Land* and *Mauberley*. For these lyrical monologues the essential fiction is the dualism of inside-consciousness and outside-consciousness, again represented by the closed circle of lyric and the continuous, historically informed flow of the dramatic monologue. Figures like Tiresias and Mauberley sustain this fiction by appearing to overcome it. Without their guidance we could enter neither poem, since we would lack the sustaining illusion of the poem as a consciousness that requires entry.

Fictional schemes such as the dualism or the binary opposition foster poetry in ways precluded by more rigidly analytical intellectual constructs. Pound and Eliot were alert to the fluid but sometimes palpable distinction between poetic and intellectual demands on language, and were willing to borrow the rhetorical strategies of more rigorous analyses to further nonrational uses of language, but those aren't the primary concern here. Pound was well aware that the immediate postwar situation presented an unutterable complexity of available aesthetic modes, but he had to schematize the situation. His plan, in part, was to incriminate contemporary culture for its failure to foster the most finely wrought forms of art by linking that indifference to the ignorant violence and sacrifice of war. Equally important, he attempted to develop in the worldview of his persona a limited group of aesthetic choices, each of which, historically, led to oblivion.

One problem any discussion of *Mauberley* faces is its relation to the *Cantos,* already well under way by 1919. If *Mauberley* rejects poetic modes and poetic voices developed by Pound in London while the *Cantos* look forward to his life on the continent and to new modes of poetic and aesthetic experience, what does this suggest about the voice and structure of the apparently more conventional poem? The *Cantos,* three of which appeared in *Poetry* in 1917, introduce a distinct method of composition, one peculiarly collage-like and more divergent from the aesthetic Pound derived from Browning and the medieval romance poets. Yet in 1919–20 he hadn't become entirely at ease with his new project. The original three *Cantos* would be disassembled and reordered, much of them discarded in the process. In turning to the composition of *Hugh Selwyn Mauberley* immediately after *Homage to Sextus Propertius,* a farewell of a different kind, Pound consciously sought to bury—with some praise—the poet he had been.

Mauberley, who is not a character in the way that Andrea Del Sarto is, rejects the Pound of "troublesome energies," as Pound noted for the benefit of future critics (Connolly, 59). Mauberley buries Pound, but for the purposes of this poem neither Pound nor Mauberley need be explicitly identified with the living Ezra Pound who was about to bid "farewell to London." Instead, these figures are conflicting aesthetic dynamics. E.P. is a dynamic too energetic for this conventionally ordered poem, with its lyrical and monologic temperament, to contain; he is already immersed in the *Cantos* and is packing his bag for Paris and a Joycean commitment to language as an expanding universe. The Mauberley in Pound lingers over the wreckage of London life, the aesthetic of which he has already more or less abandoned. My argument thus far differs from that of William Spanos, who searches valiantly for a critical unity (and finds it), in that I don't agree that the poem "must be interpreted as Mauberley's terminal judgment of himself and his age" (75), but argue rather that to draw a line between a "fictional character" named Mauberley and an actual poet named Ezra Pound obfuscates the poem's attempt to confront a deep division of purpose and psyche. The speaker's assumption of the role of witness rather than of participant (witness even of his own demise) suggests how Pound in a few years would schematically edit *The Waste Land* with its similar testimonial voice. But Spanos is essentially correct, I believe, in his conclusion that "with Elpenor purged Pound is fully freed from his dalliance with Circe to resume his Odyssean voyage—*The Cantos*" (96).

Dating *Mauberley* with precision presents the problem of aligning it with the early *Cantos* and the criticism Pound was writing at the time. Pound published the sequence in its entirety in June 1920, with none of the sections having previously appeared in periodicals. He dated the "Mauberley" subsequence "1920," while "Envoi," immediately preceding "Mauberley," is dated "1919." Yet this last date is an afterthought. In the manuscript (at Hamilton College) "1919" is written by hand on a typescript of "Envoi" that appears to be a final draft. Of course, this does not mean the date is spurious; it merely suggests that the significance of dating this section came late to Pound. At least two typewriters produced the typescript—one with a characteristic partly dropped capital *C,* the other, used for "E.P. Ode Pour l'election de son Sepulchre" with a normal *C* but a heavy lowercase *s.* Also, at least two different ribbons appear. But what does this tell us? "Envoi," dated 1919, appears to have been typed on the same machine with the same ribbon as "Mauberley I," dated 1920. The dates may be arbitrary; the history in the poem is allegorical fiction, like all temporal movement in poetry, necessary not for actual historical reasons but to sustain the illusion of movement between the poles of aesthetic dialectic.

The poem is an open-ended sequence and postulates any number of reiterations of its pluralistic structure. Further reiteration would not change that loose structure, only further confirm its continuity. The individual sections embrace the discontinuous closed circle of lyric, but critics who have tried to read the sequence in unreconstructed New Critical fashion to find some compelling idea of form to which they might attribute complementary moral and ethic structures have consistently failed, to my mind, to satisfactorily describe the poem. We can see how this continuous—and potentially unending—coupling of discontinuous lyrics works by contrasting *Hugh Selwyn Mauberley* with the *Cantos* Pound wrote in the same period. *Mauberley,* in comparison with the struggle for new form in the *Cantos,* seems to settle too easily for lyric closure in the individual sections and yet to resist any larger internal drive for coherence. But although Mauberley neither uncritically embraces the self-affirming structure of narrative nor extends the principle of lyric closure to the whole, this does not demonstrate that it has no structure at all; rather its structure refuses the very burden of moral design the poem invites us to assume, and refuses the certainties of conventional form without offering, as the *Cantos* do, the consolation of newer, though unperfected, ideas of form and structure derived from Whitman and other avant-garde sources. But the actual structure of *Mauberley* derives from Browning and Henry James (as Pound himself noted [1950, 180]), based not on the pairing of poems, repetitions of thematic statements, or reechoes of aesthetic motifs but simply on the modulations of the dominant voice. As Ronald Bush has said, "Pound wrote *Mauberley* while the *Cantos* were on the back burner in order to compete, for once, with the novelists on their own terms" (262)—especially, I would add, to compete with their assured use of narrative consciousness.

The *Cantos* weren't entirely out of Pound's mind, though. He had already begun to reconsider and expand the Imagiste aesthetic in the first three *Cantos* drafted in 1915 and published in *Poetry* in 1917 (Bush, 23–24). This expansion toward Vorticism reintroduced larger ideas of structure into his poetry and helped make *Mauberley* possible. He continued to write *Cantos* while he worked on *Homage to Sextus Propertius* and *Hugh Selwyn Mauberley.* On December 13, 1919, he wrote to his father, "Have done Cantos 5, 6, and 7, each more incomprehensible than the one preceding it; don't know what's to be done about it" (Papers, Yale). And in the spring of 1920 he sent his father advance sheets of *Mauberley,* which he referred to as his "new poems." The plural construction suggests that, like the *Cantos, Mauberley* is a sequence, not a monolithic entity. The *Cantos,* Pound quickly demonstrated in his rewriting of the first three, would be pliable and open-ended too, and if that mock epic seems an uneasy mixture of old and new poetics (though thematically committed to bidding the old aesthetic goodbye), that is due to Pound's growing interest in a more encyclopedic form, his continued regard for James, his attempts to come to terms with Whitman, and his fascination with Joyce's *Ulysses,* which he had followed carefully, proofread, and promoted as it appeared episode by episode until the Nausicaa episode was firmly suppressed and Margaret Anderson prosecuted and fined in 1920.

Pound was discomfited when halfway through the book Joyce abandoned what Pound took to be the ultimate extension of Flaubert's realism. He always discussed *Ulysses* as the culmination of that tradition rather than, as Eliot saw it, a spatial, symbolic recasting of a classical quest-myth. But the early episodes clearly enthralled Pound. As early as 1918 he wrote of *Ulysses,* "His profoundest work, most significant. . . . *Ulysses,* obscure, even obscene, as life itself is obscene in places, but an impassioned meditation on life" (1966, 139). Pound here remains committed to an aesthetic of realism ("Obscene, as life itself is obscene"); in fact, I doubt that he ever came to see *Ulysses* (or the *Cantos,* for that matter) as primarily self-reflexive, despite their high degree of ironic self-consciousness, since in his later years he grew more and more committed to a utilitarian, socially active aesthetic, which he seemed to believe the *Cantos* manifested; but his practice after his confrontation with *Ulysses* was to produce poetry that rejected an a priori commitment to form, a poetry resolutely continuous, ironically self-conscious and self-referential, and one that in the end subsumes—whatever its creator's wishes—the temporal allegory of history in an argument privileging process over product.

Chronology may help establish the simultaneity of Pound's apparently conflicting aesthetics of this period. Joyce published *Portrait of the Artist as a Young Man* in England on February 12, 1917, launched by a review in *The Egoist* (1917a, 21–22) in which Pound claimed that "James Joyce produces the nearest thing to Flaubertian prose that we now have in English." The original "Canto I" appeared in *Poetry* in June 1917. "Canto II" appeared the next month, and "Canto III" followed in the August issue. These first three Cantos were noticeably indebted to Browning. When Pound rewrote them he exorcized not only Browning but most traces of linear or temporal development, yet without imposing lyric closure.

Joyce sent the first two episodes of *Ulysses* to Pound for *The Little Review* in December 1917. Pound's comment (cited in *The Little Review*) was "It looks to me rather better than Flaubert." For the next three years Pound proofread *Ulysses.* The first episode appeared in *The Little Review* in March 1918 and continued until the September–December 1920 issue, when the journal was prosecuted. *The Egoist* in 1919 published fragments of four episodes, but the magazine's printer objected to it, and eventually refused to set type for it.

"The Fourth Canto," published in the June 1920 issue of *The Dial,* is entirely committed to a structural openness of the sort Joseph Frank has called "spatial form," and which many of Pound's readers, following Pound's 1933 suggestion, have called "ideogramic" (Bush, 14). However, as Bush has convincingly argued, applying the term "ideogramic" to the early *Cantos* distorts literary history and Pound's aesthetic development, and even if applied to the later *Cantos* the term may "distort our perception of the *Cantos* so that a structural device [will seem] more prominent than the form of the whole" (15). My contention is that the *Cantos* resist all of Pound's received conceptions of form (that is, that it be linear, narrative, temporal, Browningesque, lyric, and Flaubertian) and substitute synchronicity, flux, and open-endedness not as a lack of form but as a rejection of the application to literary structures of the metaphor of form. In *Mauberley* the commitment to a dialectic of conventional forms does not extend to the sequence as a whole; rather it is localized in issues of stanza, line, and sentence; the *Cantos* would restrict formal commitment still further, at times rejecting even the single phrase as a formal unit.

As already noted, Pound had sent his father copies of Cantos V–VII in December 1919, by which time he most likely had written part of *Mauberley,* perhaps the entire first section. The writing of the *Cantos* and the writing of the various sections of *Mauberley* therefore overlapped. Certainly the new aesthetic displayed in the fourth through seventh Cantos was well-established before June 1920 when the Ovid Press published *Hugh Selwyn Mauberley* in an edition of 200 copies. And it seems reasonable to assume that the finished drafts of Cantos IV–VII, the revised versions of the first three, and *Mauberley* all postdate the impact of the early episodes of *Ulysses.* The doubts Pound felt about the Sirens (1966, 160) and later episodes may parallel certain doubts he felt about the *Cantos,* which he ceased to work on from late 1919 until early 1922 ("Canto VIII" appeared in *The Dial* in May 1922)—doubts that the *Cantos* themselves suggest grew from a nostalgia for the linear temporal aesthetic of epic and narrative he (and Joyce) had abandoned.

However, if the open-ended and self-referential structure of *Mauberley* eschews a linear temporality it does not preclude the idea of argument. In fact, like the arguments of *The Waste Land* (as demonstrated by John Xiros Cooper), *Ulysses,* and eventually the *Cantos,* the argument of *Hugh Selwyn Mauberley* to a large degree displaces form, even in a sense becomes form.

What I mean by argument is what Laurence Lerner means by it, "The framework which would be common both to the poem and to a paraphrase of it" (50). Argument then is the logical or cognitive structure of the poem, and its relationship to form is complex and variable. New Criticism would argue that argument and form are mutual determinants, and that their coincidence, in whatever terms they can be made to coincide, is the mark of unity and a sign of the poem's quality. Such strained conjecture risks the fallacy of treating the poem as a natural object, an error especially dangerous in dealing with poetry of such highly ironic self-awareness. The efforts of critics to demonstrate such unity in *Mauberley* has led some to conclude that their failure coincides with the failure of the poem, that the very open-ended quality of the poem is a weakness rather than a characteristic that requires further investigation.

Certainly, replication is not necessarily the first virtue we expect in a poem, and *Mauberley* cannot replicate endlessly, not on its original terms. For one thing, the Mauberley voice speaks its own elegy. That it does so at least twice does not mean it can do so forever, since the poems diminish in scope and rhetorical insistence as the sequence proceeds. In this particular way form and argument do coincide. In the modulated elegy of section IV of part 2 the speaker has reduced his self-summary to mere epitaph:

> "I was
> And I no more exist;
> Here drifted
> An hedonist."

Like all self-elegies, however, this is too self-mocking to accept as other than a critique of the elegiac mode. Unsurprisingly, the voice of this supposedly departed hedonist continues (though no longer quoting itself) into "Medallion," where it rather arbitrarily concludes. A further elegy would be still more minimal, but Pound's aesthetic, here and later, refuses the more extreme forms of minimalism.

Before continuing with *Mauberley,* however, I want to consider briefly the aesthetic of the *Cantos* and the way it develops from the original I–III through the more characteristic (as we now think of them) Cantos V–VII, an aesthetic evolving in the same period in which Pound wrote *Mauberley.* This may illuminate the aesthetic tension working in Pound in this period, and may explain why faint traces of linearity survive in a poem that otherwise almost explicitly rejects the sort of development Pound sometimes seemed to admire in Browning and in the prose narratives of Henry James.

The original "Canto I" opens with an explicit reference to Browning (which Pound retained for the opening lines of the revised "Canto II"), and goes on to explain what he wants from Browning's aesthetic, which he, Pound, is borrowing:

> Hang it all, there can be but one *Sordello!*
> But say I want to, say I take your whole bag of tricks,
> Let in your quirks and tweeks, and say the thing's an
>   art-form,
> Your *Sordello,* and that the modern world
> Needs such a rag-bag to stuff all its thought in.
> Say that I dump my catch, shiny and silvery
> As fresh sardines flapping and slipping on the marginal
>   cobbles?
> (I stands before the booth, the speech; but the truth
> is inside this discourse—this booth is full of the
>   marrow of wisdom.)
> Give up th' intaglio method. (1917b, 113)

In revising this opening passage Pound retained (in the new "Canto II") only the first line, which he then addressed to Browning by name. From there the Canto enters the open-ended associative argument characteristic of the poems as we now know them:

> Hang it all, Robert Browning,
> There can be but the one "Sordello."
> But Sordello, and my Sordello?
> Lo Sordels si fo di Mantovana.
> So-Shu churned in the sea.
> Seal sports in the spray-whited circles of cliff-wash,
> Sleek head, daughter of Lir,
>   eyes of Picasso
> Under black fur-hood, lithe daughter of Ocean.

In the 1917 *Poetry,* the *Cantos* are relatively linear in their argument and no more freely associative than much of Pound's other work of this period. In revising them Pound dropped much explicitly connective tissue and opened them up to a freer aesthetic of juxtaposition. Conventional ideas of closure and unity signify less here than the logic of compression, association, the unconscious, simultaneity, and spatial relationship, all of which preclude the linear argument of narrative and even of much conventional lyric.

All this is familiar to readers of the *Cantos.* But *Mauberley,* as I've suggested, looks as though it should still retain a linear argument, if not linear temporality: the stanzas are nearly regular, at least in most sections, the rhymes are familiar—except for those in which Greek is made to rhyme with English—and the poem generally seems to invite a conventional reading based on the expectations we would bring to a ballad or a Browning monologue. However, while those expectations are fulfilled by strictly local effects it should be obvious that these will not serve well the larger functions of the poem. The voice is not a conventional Browning monologue voice, nor two or more such voices. It is a voice that is beyond omniscience, one of the sort that Hugh Kenner, discussing *Ulysses* (and borrowing from David Hayman) calls the "Arranger" (1987, 61). In *Ulysses,* as at times in the *Cantos,* this voice clearly is one of self-reflexivity, and represents a mind that "arranges" the work *as a literary work.* This kind of fictional voice differs from that of the usual omniscient narrator, and to separate one from the other throughout the *Cantos* would be a daunting task. But in *Mauberley* this voice dominates the poem, speaking not as a witness to events as such but to the literary event in question, the formation or recover of aesthetics from the rubble of the second decade of this century and the third and fourth of Pound's life.

The first poem of the first section, entitled "E.P. Ode Pour l'election de son Sepulchre," opens with a linear narrative betrayed only by the title ("E.P." is clearly an afterthought: Pound vacillated about including it) and the judgmental point of view. The argument of this poem—and several others in the sequence—is at odds with the point of view and voice of the sequence as a whole in that its very simplicity leads us to expect a Browning narrator of conventional omniscience, an expectation that goes unfilled. Pound's insistence that Mauberley speaks the whole seems irrational, since no such readily designated narrator is likely to speak of himself in the third person, as he does—or seems to—in the second half of the sequence. The poem simply confounds our usual expectations of narrative unity. Reading it without such expectations (and dismissing Pound's troublesome late-life clues) we find no difficulty in following the thread. The arguments are several, and though overlapped at times in a somewhat disconcerting way, are relatively clear. E.P. is dead and buried after three years of trying to "resuscitate the dead art of poetry," possibly to attempt again the "pure poetry" of the 1890s but with a touch of realism borrowed from Flaubert, the realism of literature, not of life. But the age in which he lived—a restless, destructive, warlike era—had no time for him and his art or that of his fellow craft-laborers. Instead, the best of a whole generation went to war to save what they thought was civilization but in fact was only its shell.

To see what happened to that civilization the poem looks back at several generations attempting to purify their art, beginning with the Pre-Raphaelites. In their era the separation between art and civilization had already begun. It worsened in the 1890s, so that the falsehood that Lionel Johnson died by falling from a stool in a pub seems a particularly appropriate because so degraded form of myth. The various characters of the era—Brennbaum, Mr. Nixon (probably Arnold Bennett), the "stylist" (certainly Ford Madox Ford), and women patrons of arts that have ceased to function—seem to characterize the situation as the practical E.P. understood it. His "Envoi" sent his "dumb born" book forth to his muse, the undying figure of beauty. The poem now focuses (a year later— "Envoi" dated 1919, "Mauberley" 1920) on the limited role that remains for the man of genuine poetic passion, that of the miniaturist. Epic died with E.P., which means Epic Poetry as much as Ezra Pound; all that remains is the small poem, the quick sketch in profile, and this is not enough to sustain life or civilization. Though Flaubert remains the true Penelope, the only love left to this diminished poet-figure is the engraver's. And clearly the engraver is not the sort of artist we expect to reconstruct an entire world (Achaia). Looking again at the three years of E.P.'s attempted resuscitation, the arranger concludes that in that time the poet-figure "drank ambrosia"—that is, he numbed his senses to the earthquakes about him, little realizing that his previous conception of art was inadequate to the real task at hand. Eventually, he discovered this ("The Age Demanded") and withdrew, unable to link the failure of the indi-

vidual to the failure of the state. In retreat from "neo-Nietzschean chatter" he inhabited a tropical place of voluntary isolation, a state of being
that as it became more central to him made inevitable his "final / exclu-
sion from the world of letters." Thus isolated, the poet-figure speaks for
himself the brief epitaph previously quoted, and the poem closes with
the finely wrought poem "Medallion" that some critics have insisted represents the failure of Mauberley's aesthetic but is actually a graceful sum-
mation of the truncated, overly purified lyric aesthetic to which the poem
bids farewell. That aesthetic excluded E.P. (epic poetry) from the start,
since history was the primary impurity the poets of the 1890s sought to
purge, and which the events of the early twentieth century demonstrated
that poetry had to incorporate or become irrelevant. Ezra Pound wasn't
wrong from the start, but his aesthetic, which was closely linked to the
Pre-Raphaelites and the poets of the 1890s, excluded epic, and fell prey
to the tendency of the age to relegate art to lesser status than war, for
example, or making money.

So Pound clears the way for a new aesthetic, one that would make
the *Cantos* possible. This new aesthetic prescribes a fresh way of regard-
ing voice, structure, form, argument, and narration. It would show "the
full smile" rather than restricting itself to "art / in profile." *Mauberley* is an
important step in that process, not only as *ars poetica* but as the first embodiment of the voice that would become the dominant one of the *Cantos.*

Where, most specifically, can we identify this voice, which I have
already noted is one that rather than maintaining the fiction of being a
real voice in an actual world betrays its consciousness of being the voice
of a literary work? It is the voice that directs the poem rather than actually speaking it, a voice Pound uses clearly but rather crudely at the beginning of the original "Canto I":

> But say I want to, say I take your whole bag of tricks,
> Let in your quirks and tweeks, and say the things's an
> art form

and more subtly in the new "Canto I" in the interjection

> Lie quiet Divius. I mean, that is Andreas Divius,
> In officina Wecheli, 1538, out of Homer.

The awareness of the poem as a literary act distinguishes this voice from that of Odysseus and all the other personae in the *Cantos:* it is the voice of the poet-as-arranger, the poet actually making a poem, and it is almost a new voice in poetry, though it is not new in the novel and is characteristic of the genre to which *Tristram Shandy, Moby-Dick,* and *Ulysses* belong, a genre in which literary praxis is part of the fictional ethos.

In the *Cantos* the voice of the arranger is distinct from the voices of the various historical personae, but in *Hugh Selwyn Mauberley* it blends almost insensibly with the ordinary voice of third-person narration, which in turn modulates readily with the novelistic first-person voices of "'Siena Mi Fe'; Disfecemi Maremma," and "Mr. Nixon," but remains distinct from the more conventionally literary first-person voice of "Envoi (1919)." When the arranger speaks clearly he assumes the stance of a critic; his phrases are measured, qualified, and suspicious of extravagance:

> Wrong from the start—
> No, hardly . . .
>
> * * *
> The age demanded an image
> Of its accelerated grimace
>
> * * *
> Nature receives him;
> With a placid and uneducated mistress
> He exercises his talents
> And the soil meets his distress.
>
> * * *
> The glow of porcelain
> Brought no reforming sense
> To his perception
> Of the social inconsequence.

The difficulty with *Mauberley,* then, is that a search for an overriding persona—either Pound or Mauberley—is misdirected. The consciously literary voice shapes the poem, and it is a critical, not a dramatic voice. The great originality of *Mauberley* is in separating the literary voice from the voices of the personae and using it to consider the fate of two aesthete-poets who are clearly personae (masked voices) of Pound's lyric and dramatic-historical aesthetics, aspects of his creative self as it would wander, suffer, and fade if unchecked by this same critical voice. The latter, by virtue of its literary self-awareness, can impose the irony of distance lacking in the simple (and genuinely engaging) contemplation of beauty. To "fish by obstinate isles" is eventually to drift away as hedonist, and both E.P. (Ezra Poetry, Epic Pound) and His Majesty's Ship, Hugh Selwyn Mauberley, are prone to drifting off on voyages of indeterminate if purposeful duration.

As Pound embarked on his endless voyage into history he bid farewell to London in his most self-critical poem, but in a voice that makes the *Cantos* possible, the voice of literary awareness that knows that for literature to redeem itself and culture to thrive it cannot lose itself in empathy but must stand back and critically direct an enterprise that otherwise would drift into hedonism or chaos. Pound and Eliot devised their rhetorical strategies from a somewhat elitist idea of the discourse-community, but their powerful sense of the social and psychological implications of language-politics is one of the sources of their continuing cultural and aesthetic power.

Lowell

Autobiography and Vulnerability

In 1977, reviewing for *Salmagundi* magazine "thirty years" of his own poetry, Robert Lowell observed that "the thread that strings it together is my autobiography, it is a small scale *Prelude,* written in many different styles and with digression, yet a continuing story—still wayfaring" (1977b, 113). Wordsworth's *Prelude,* a lengthy blank-verse narrative, uses appropriate dramatic devices and narrative strategies to retell, revise, and partly conceal a carefully orchestrated version of the author's life, the "growth of a poet's mind." Lowell's poems, on the other hand, are brief dramatic monologues or interior monologues, wrought by an essentially lyric sensibility, so his self-description challenges the convention of life-telling as storytelling and implies that the "thread," the absent unifying narrative, is not a textual function but a conspiracy of the poet's intention and the reader's expectations. His autobiography is not what he has written but what lingers uninscribed in the background.

Autobiographical intention and expectation reside in Lowell's aesthetic, however, suggesting how far he has diverged from the poetics and critical requirements of Eliot (as he was usually read through the 1950s), Crane, and especially John Crowe Ransom and Allen Tate. Lowell's originality, though, does not lie in his revival of the autobiographical spirit of Wordsworth but in his sense of how fiction informs life-telling, and how problematic is the relationship between the will to express and the "sound of words" actually generated. Like Stevens, Lowell finds the tension between imagination and reality a rich source of emotional and intellectual imperatives, but also a point of terrible mutual pressures. Simultaneously maintaining so weighty and arbitrary a binary opposition and attempting to negotiate it is the burden these poets have inherited from Western culture, but it is also the source of their differing poetics.

Lacking Stevens's or Eliot's enormous range of rhetorical strategies, Lowell focuses his energies on a particular device that after 1957 would remain central to his poetic. The "trope of vulnerability" inscribes the mutual pressure of reality and imagination in partly audible form. Centered in this ambiguous trope, Lowell's poems both generate and challenge an uninscribed or only partly inscribed autobiography that relies more on the reader's instinct for authorial intention and the conventions of reading than on direct exposition. In *The Dolphin* the complex layers of fiction and historical accuracy blend in a disconcerting way. But in the earlier *Life Studies* Lowell uses an elegantly written prose sketch to suggest the novelistic underpinnings of his project.

Life Studies

To prepare the reader for the unfamiliar, highly personal verse monologues at the core of his book, Lowell early in *Life Studies* juxtaposes a lengthy fragment of prose autobiography with poetry of a decidedly autobiographical cast that still retains the privileges of concealment and subversion characteristic of the genres of lyric or dramatic monologue. "91 Revere Street" attempts to assert not only the presence but the actuality of the writer—not merely as speaker, but as a subjective self with the power to speak for itself, distinct from the conventionalized, restricted persona of the literary work.

Lowell rejects one set of conventions only to embrace, through indirection, a second set—the conventions of autobiography—which are fluid and intersect in various ways with those of the meditative poem. But self-representation occurs differently in different genres, and Lowell is well aware that the complexities of voice in the modern era, whether in fiction or in autobiography, resist the determinism of convention. Emerson's more comprehensive and decidedly nonempirical vision of the self may answer more strongly than Freud's to the problem of how the ego of the artist embraces the sometimes mutually exclusive worlds of memory, history, and imagination. He suggests in "History" and "The Poet" (and elsewhere in his work) that the concept of a self is so pervasive as to define every form of discourse without, in turn, being universally or totally defined.

"91 Revere Street" contrasts the relatively slack freedom of prose expression, with its license to maunder and relax, to the psychologically as well as aesthetically demanding compression of verse monologues and lyrics that so strongly resemble the prose piece in language, theme, and situation. Lowell needs to assert the consciousness of self that, as Georges Gusdorf points out, is an essential precondition for autobiography (30). This consciousness of self, an awareness of one's personality, is, as T.S. Eliot implies in his famous statement about personality and emotions, precisely what the writer who gladly embraces the conventions of fiction or the lyric may hope to escape (1951, 21). In Lowell's autobiographical prose, abutted to his poetry, the assertion of presence as consciousness rather than as construct attempts to link more intimately the fictional texts to the ordinary worlds of the writer and the reader. This is a paradoxical intention, since to succeed in it would call into question the efficacy of the fictional text. Lowell is aware of this paradox and exploits it.

The language of this autobiographical fragment does not differ in kind from the language of the partly fictionalized first-person verse-monologues it introduces. Linguistic critics have decisively refuted the idea that poetry or fiction wields a special or discrete language, so genre theory cannot demonstrate that particular genres generate languages differing in some essential way from the language of ordinary discourse. The prose autobiography differs in form and rhetoric from the poem or romance, but its relationship to whatever is not made of language is equally tenuous and arbitrary. Even structural differences are tentative. Crossing formal though arbitrary boundaries, many of Lowell's poems in *Life Studies* derive from prose sketches originally intended like "91 Revere Street" to be part of a longer prose autobiography. The poems are condensed rather than abridged from the prose and retain many of the structural characteristics of the prose passages (for instance, compare "Terminal Days at Beverly Farms" [1959, 73] with the corresponding passage in "Near the Unbalanced Aquarium" [1987, 354]). Lowell had no hesitation about crossing generic boundaries this way because he felt that prose and poetry had much to learn from each other. In an interview he said that "on the whole, prose is less cut off from life than poetry is," and argued that Chekhov or Tolstoy might offer more to the contemporary poet than many poetic models (1987, 244). Later in the same interview he recalled, "When I was working on *Life Studies* I found I had no language or meter that would allow me to approximate what I saw or remembered. Yet in prose I had already found what I wanted, the conventional style of auto-biography and reminiscence. So I wrote my autobiographical poetry in a style I thought I had discovered in Flaubert, one that used images and ironic or amusing particulars" (1987, 244).

Lowell uses a prose sketch to establish his psychological and emotional commitment to the more highly fictionalized poems that follow. Through this personal gesture he implies dramatic continuity between distinct genres and lends the lyric monologue the authenticity of witnessed history and attested feeling. The historical elements invoked in his sketch (some of which are carried over, in variously modified forms, into the poems) include an ancient portrait, knickknacks, furniture, and other artifacts that point to the speaker's minor but actual role in local and family sagas. These familial, ancestral, and local objects assume a life of their own: independent, to the extent that they can be so depicted, from the author's feelings, yet actually significant because rendered in the particular terms of his sensibility. At the same time Lowell implicitly rejects the positivist approach of literary naturalism.

Further, Lowell in his autobiographical sketch invokes a Dickensian exteriority to present characters somewhat exaggerated or larger than life, including his own father as well as Commander Billy Harkness. The presence of these comic figures gives the sketch a satiric edge that contrasts with the tragic melodrama of poems such as "My Last Afternoon with Uncle Devereaux Winslow," in which the tonal muting of Winslow as he declines toward death infects the child with a lassitude inappropriate to his years. Tonal shifts dislocate the reader and undermine the conventions of autobiography, the interior monologue, and the elegy. The studied prose of "91 Revere Street" plants expectations of a literary formality the loose free verse poems, despite their solemn topics, deny.

"91 Revere Street" opens with an elaborate discussion of the concealments of art, in this instance a portrait of an ancestor, Major Mordecai Myers, whose name is partially withheld by another ancestor's privately printed *Biographical Sketches* (1959, 11). As Helen Deese has pointed out, this portrait closes the sketch, too, as Billy Harkness sits under it teasing the child's parents with his brash, manly humor (182–83). The nature of biography, and autobiography as well, Lowell's sketch demonstrates, is to play with revelation, but in the end to accede to concealment. The father of Mordecai Myers is even more concealed, "given neither name nor initial," and the portrait of the younger Myers, labeled Major Mordecai Myers, is partially a fiction, since Myers was a major only by courtesy (1959, 11). Life-details abound, yet critical items, including name and rank, are suspect. Finally, we learn that "Major Mordecai Myers' portrait has been mislaid past finding," so like the cloth scarlet letter of Hawthorne's Custom House sketch this fragment of empirical evidence has passed into the realm of fiction. It remains symptomatic, though. The author has fixed it in the mind, along with the house on Revere Street, "where it survives all the distortions of fantasy, all the blank befogging of forgetfulness." Yet it is *only* in the mind that it survives. The mind, Lowell explains, reorders to give significance to *things* that in mere actuality would lack purpose. In memory, "each is in its place, each has its function, its history, its drama. There, all is preserved by that motherly care that one either ignored or resented in his youth. The things and their owners come back urgent with life and meaning—because finished, they are endurable and perfect" (13). Lowell's argument about the use of fiction is clear: fiction lends life, meaning, and order to an otherwise incomplete, unsatisfying quotidian existence. Its divorce from actuality is blessedly absolute—though much of Lowell's poetic project from *Life Studies* on would be dedicated to blurring the distinction between fact and fiction, life and art. Here Lowell makes no explicit appeal for a more sophisticated reading of his work, as he later would in *The Dolphin* and *Day by Day,* but he amply hints that autobiography is not a naturalistic presentation of what once actually occurred. Rather it is a highly selective and ordered fantasy of language-empowerment in which "things" whose referents seem real assume the decidedly unreal sheen of durability and perfection.

Persons, too, linked to their "things," assume meaning that presumably in life they lacked or could not express. Cousin Cassie's life is an example of one partly under erasure, since her brief mention in Lowell's sketch merely records that she died in 1922 and left a vast number and variety of "things" to empower Lowell's memory and narrative. These emblematic objects foreshadow others, such as the "rhinoceros hide" chair Lowell's father loves. But the primary object in this tale is the house itself, which embodies the author's frustrations, ambitions, and, to some extent, personal history. In a sense an edifice is a secret place, like the mind, in which tales begin. Though the Lowell character is fictionally reconstituted as a child, his preternatural sensitivity to his surroundings and his willingness to eavesdrop on his parents and report to the reader what he heard (even though at first he can hardly make out the words, which he renders as "Weelawaugh, we-ee-eelawaugh," "But-and, but-and, but and!" [19]) suggests that even at this early age the act of narration was intrinsic to the shaping of his world.

Major Myers in every way is a tame and unromantic ancestor, except for being a Jewish member of one of America's most prominent WASP families. Lowell makes little of this Jewishness (in life, Lowell was fascinated by Jewish ancestry, whether his own or that of others), though the child imagines Myers as that cruel anti-Semitic archetype, the Wandering Jew. Far from being motivated by bigotry, the child wants to discover a viable model of the outsider, one his more immediate family lacks, except in the improbable figure of Amy Lowell. Myers is not a very appealing model, but his outsider status, however mildly depicted, makes him a fascinating example for the child-poet who wishes to portray himself as an outlaw of sorts.

Depicting the protagonist as outsider or potential outsider is one of the most common strategies of autobiography. Presumably, anyone sharply distinguished by his or her presence in an autobiography has already set himself or herself apart; but Lowell's strategies for distinguishing outsideness from inside-ness are worth considering. The child Lowell, tortured by conflicting desires for social acceptance and eccentric individuality, resorts to peculiar devices to distinguish himself from his surroundings, such as his torture of Eric Burckhard (whom he calls a "Lake Geneva Spider Monkey") when the child is ill with mumps, and more tellingly his longing to abandon his unsatisfactory identity as a small boy and become a slightly older girl so that he can feel more important in the Brimmer Street School hierarchy (22). This apparent desire for conformity strains the child's vision of his future. He cannot imagine himself as an adult male, since he lacks a role model for that age ("I was quite without hero worship for my father," he tells us [13]). The status quo is unacceptable: "To be a boy at Brimmer was to be small, denied, and weak"; yet he cannot look forward to his eventual enrollment at St. Mark's: "I distrusted change, knew each school since kindergarten had been more constraining and punitive than its predecessor" (28).

Outsider status is a state every child experiences, one that as Lowell depicts it engenders a passion for conformity greater than any adult feels. The children at Brimmer worry most about their relative popularity, which is patently ephemeral. Since the girls continue past the fourth grade, while boys have to transfer to another school, Lowell in his desire to stay put (to "soak there all morning like a bump on a log," as a teacher puts it [30]) lies to his mother, claiming that the headmistress has "begged" him to stay (30). Finally, this conflict between a growing sense of being outside and a rage for acceptance breaks out in violence. The child Lowell "bloodied Bulldog Binney's nose against the pedestal of George Washington's statue in full view of Commonwealth Avenue" (31). After several other depredations the young thug is expelled from the Public Garden and the story returns to the Revere Street house to focus on the adult world.

In characteristic bildungsroman style Lowell represents his protagonist engaged in the conflict between individual development and the desire to conform to a familiar and therefore unchallenging social context. Outsider status is not earned, it is intrinsic, and rather than reveling in his individuality the child is desperately trying to avoid it. Rather than waiting for fate, the child in irrational rage precipitates the turning point in his story. This comes when young Lowell decides to become an outlaw and oppose the easy conformity of school life. This ruse, which severs him from the comforts as well as the strictures of school life, allows him to turn more frankly to the problem of the available but unsatisfactory adult role models in his life.

After the violence in the Public Garden the Brimmer Street School disappears from the sketch, which then centers on a new character. Billy Harkness embodies an easygoing nonconformity that is Dickensian, comic, and a clear alternative to the tense indecision of the father and the shrill antagonism of the mother. But the child recedes in this part of the sketch. His role is now that of the Jamesian observer, and only after long passages describing the antics of Harkness, who made both of his parents somewhat uncomfortable, does he return to the subject of his own feelings. He notes that in recording these Sunday dinner conversations he may "exaggerate their embarrassment because they hover so grayly in recollection." More strikingly, because he recognizes their literary value, he notes that these dinners as he has depicted them, "seem to anticipate ominously my father's downhill progress as a civilian and a Bostonian" (43). Such foreshadowing characterizes fiction not life, though we have

learned in life to use what we discover in fiction. Even the act of notic-
ing, in retrospect, that these dinners *seemed* to foreshadow worse things is
a literary act.

Having broached the subject of his feelings again, the protagonist
returns to the oppressive presence of things. Lowell finds objects sentient
with meaning, but only with the authority of interpretation and experience does that meaning escape the insignificance of material positivism.
The inherited furniture in the Revere Street house unpleasantly affects
the child Lowell by engaging his powers of personification: "I used to sit
through the Sunday dinners absorbing cold and anxiety from the table. I
imagined myself hemmed in by our new, inherited Victorian Myers furniture. . . . Here, table, highboy, chairs, and screen—mahogany, cherry,
teak, looked nervous and disproportioned. They seemed to wince, touch
elbows, shift from foot to foot" (43). The insistence on the allegorical
sentience of the furniture suggests that we are dealing with literature not
life. The child may actually have felt oppressed by the furniture, but voicing that discomfort through personification is a literary act. And like
foreshadowing, such voicing requires some degree of literary sophistica-
tion—that is, the ability to make metaphors and similes. Lowell is preparing his readers for a series of poems covering the years from a period
preceding the Revere Street sketch to middle age. To establish a Jamesian
child's voice intelligent enough to plausibly see the world as a linked
series of metaphors is part of the strategy; this is the voice of "My Last
Afternoon with Uncle Devereaux Winslow" and several other poems in
the "Life Studies" group.

Besides engendering such focused emblems as the portrait and the
forbidding furniture, "91 Revere Street" establishes a general sense of the
significance of landscape and setting. The Revere Street house is on the
"very edge of decency," as Lowell's mother says, and while Lowell describes the house in unprepossessing detail—"a flat red brick surface
unvaried by the slightest suggestion of purple panes, delicate bay, or triangular window cornice" (16)—he only briefly refers to the Italian neighborhood on which it borders. Naturally to a child the home is more
important than the larger environment, since it is the first significant site
in the individual's life.

The problem of generating larger cultural significance in one's work
is critical to writers who can take no body of myth, faith, or cultural

reference for granted. In *Life Studies* Lowell locates the beginnings of his sense of significance in the Revere Street home and on the farms at Mattapoisett and Dunbarton. Rooted in these ancestral and personal land-scapes, Lowell discovers the potential allegorical power of the ordinary material world. The transformative power of language, drawing upon the resources of the imagination, memory, and history but not the literary and religious allusions that empowered *Lord Weary's Castle,* illuminates the commonplace world of Revere Street. Resisting the examples of Eliot and Stevens—poets quite at ease with abstractions—Lowell after his first two books would base his poetic on an exacting depiction of the palpable, quotidian world (a "snapshot" aesthetic, he would ruefully call it [1977a, 127]). He would not, however, settle for being a poet merely of brilliant surfaces, if such is possible. *Life Studies* and the books that follow (including, most characteristically and comprehensively, his major long poem *History*), while avoiding transcendence through pantheistic read-ings of either the natural or the cultural world, embrace Emerson's asser-tions that "all public facts are to be individualized, all private facts are to be generalized" (246), and even more cogently, "The advancing man discovers how deep a property he has in literature—in all fable as well as in all history. He finds that the poet was no odd fellow who described strange and impossible situations, but that universal man wrote by his pen a confession true for one and true for all. His own secret biography he finds in lines wonderfully intelligible to him, dotted down before he was born" (250–51).

But one's secret biography, however universal its elements, is differ-ent than one's public autobiography. The first is revelation, but only to oneself; the other is public concealment, rhetorical manipulation, exclu-sion, editing, and fiction-making. In the process of concealment Lowell draws upon many of the strategies of realist fiction, and upon the imagis-tic resources of William Carlos Williams, with his perfectly tuned eye, rather than upon allegorical myth-making, like Stevens's, or religious meditation, like Eliot's *Four Quartets* (one of Lowell's models in the 1940s). In this combination of Chekhovian fictional strategies and imagistic ex-actitude lies Lowell's claim to significance. Illuminating rather than tran-scending the quotidian world clarifies its dimensions and deep texture, but it also exposes the complexity of our social and cultural relationships. Consequently, it exposes our individual vulnerability, guilt, and complicity, producing in Lowell's work the first truly post-Freudian poetry. In writing *History* a decade after *Life Studies* he would trace the full consequences of his poetic by reading and textually embedding his life in a broad swath of historical particulars, further advancing the idea of the "confession true for one and true for all," which is for him precisely what history is. That the acknowledgment of history constitutes a universal confession is not the least of Lowell's insights.

Rejecting the memoir, which differs from autobiography in its refusal of the exemplary mode and its casual and journalistic tone, Lowell expends on his autobiographical sketch an artistry comparable to that of his verse. This is underscored, as previously mentioned, by the fact that many of the poems in *Life Studies* were originally prose sketches similar to "91 Revere Street" that he later reworked in verse. The texture of Lowell's prose often invites the close attention commonly accorded to verse, and even a heavy-handed scholar can revise prose sentences from "91 Revere Street" into free verse nearly as vital and intense as that of "My Last Afternoon with Uncle Devereaux Winslow":

> Here, table, highboy, chairs, and screen—
> mahogany, cherry, teak—
> looked nervous and disproportioned.
> They seemed to wince, touch elbows, shift from foot to
>   foot.
> High above the highboy, our gold National Eagle
> stooped forward, plastery and doddering.
> The Sheffield silver-plate urns, more precious
> than solid sterling, peeled;
> the bodies of the heraldic mermaids
> on the Mason-Myers crest
> blushed a metallic copper tan.
>   —"91 Revere Street" (43)

> All about me
> were the works of my Grandfather's hands:
> snapshots of his *Liberty Bell* silver mine;
> his high school at *Stukkert am Neckar;*
> stogie-brown beams; fool's-gold nuggets;

octagonal red tiles,
sweaty with a secret dank, crummy with ant-stale;
a Rocky Mountain chaise longue,
its legs, shellacked saplings.
A pastel-pale Huckleberry Finn
fished with a broom straw in a basin
hollowed out of a millstone.

—"My Last Afternoon" (60)

But what is crucial is not that Lowell's prose admits rearrangement into free verse. It is that the density, texture, and self-reflexive content of his writing, whether in verse or in prose, makes the reader aware of the nature of the text, aware that a sense of literary genre, history, memory, and the self-created image of authorship empowers it.

This is not merely self-reflexiveness; the sketch has a more complex purpose, which is to outline through memory an allegorical ordering of a world that otherwise might seem too private to empower poetry. Further, as all autobiography does, this sketch serves to conceal the actual authorial self from unnecessary or digressive scrutiny by focusing the reader on aspects of the self most pertinent to the context. Lowell establishes his child-self as a reliable, observant Jamesian narrator, not as a spiritual traveler. This sketch is not a confession in the sense of Augustine's purge of guilt and self-loathing (and consequent assumption of humble righteousness), but does confess in Emerson's sense of the word by declaring the author a participant in his text. As a literary confession, "91 Revere Street" represents everyone who aspires to tell his or her own life and empower it with a significance beyond the common. Finally, by being introduced into a highly conventionalized literary context (a collection of poems), this autobiographical fragment encourages the reader to revise commonly held ideas about the reading of poetry and again reconsider the relationship between language and that which it attempts to represent.

The Dolphin

Though Lowell in the late 1950s had firmly located his poetics in an autobiographical imperative, his career continued to reshape itself in ways that sometimes startled, disappointed, or disconcerted his readers. None of his other books generated as much controversy as did *The Dolphin* when it appeared in 1973. Even before its publication, friends warned Lowell that it would arouse hostility for its frank if fragmented depiction of his domestic upheaval, his abandonment of Elizabeth Hardwick (his second wife) and his daughter, and his fathering of a child with the British novelist Caroline Blackwood. "It both fascinates and repels me," Stanley Kunitz wrote to Lowell. "Some passages I can scarcely bear to read: they are too ugly, for being too cruel, too intimately cruel" (Hamilton, 422). And Elizabeth Bishop warned Lowell not to publish, or at least to cut certain poems. She accurately perceived the high quality of the book: "I think DOLPHIN is magnificent poetry," she conceded. But as well as objecting to its "mixture of fact and fiction," she felt that "the poem— parts of it—may well be taken up and used against [Lowell] by all the wrong people" (Hamilton, 423).

Bishop was prophetic. Though *The Dolphin* would win the Pulitzer Prize, Lowell's second, the reviewers were puzzled and uncertain, and in some instances explicitly hostile, such as Adrienne Rich in a now famous attack in *American Poetry Review.* Rich called the book "cruel and shallow," and claimed that the inclusion of poems based on Elizabeth Hardwick's letters, for which Bishop also chastised Lowell, was "one of the most vindictive and mean-spirited acts in the history of poetry" (42).

Lowell's friends, well aware of the pain it would cause Hardwick to have her privacy violated and her marital dilemma made a subject of public discussion, had understandable difficulty in separating the aesthetic merits of *The Dolphin* from the muddle of Lowell's domestic life. But even now, years after the initial controversy has died down, critics generally attend to the story behind the book rather than to the story it actually tells, which is a lyrical and meditative experience rather than a narrative one. These unrhymed sonnets are elliptical, compressed, and only minimally plotted. To understand them and the sequence they form I want to consider how they challenge the conventions of autobiography by displacing historical narrative in favor of the meditative movement of the lyric. *The Dolphin* tells its story by means of reflection, analogy, contrast, and juxtaposition. The unity of the sequence derives from the accumulated sense of meditative purpose in individual sonnets and from the recurrence of related or contrasting images. Lacking the narrative grounding offered by "91 Revere Street," this sequence in some ways seems less rather than more revealing because its lack of explicit plotting places the burden of conventional historicizing upon the reader.

The half-animal and half-human figures of dolphin and mermaid suggest confrontation with the sensual and bestial sides of the speaker's psyche. The animal attraction of lust, a form of self-awareness, engenders a language of sensuality and desire. Symbolic landscapes, mostly of urban London and New York, generate a specific sense of geography. Key images, including the mermaid, the dolphin, and the fishnet at the beginning and end of the book, help give the volume unity. The imperative of *The Dolphin* is the generation of correlatives, then, and the reconciliation or deconstruction of the binary nature of these images.

By examining some characteristic sonnets I will show how Lowell's sensibility, shaped by aesthetic necessity, psychological needs, and experience, engages a wide range of material in the dynamic movement—the complexity of relationships among images and tones of voice—that give these poems their power. These late sonnets are his most extreme attempt to meld the charmed circle of lyric discontinuity with the narrative, historically aware monologue, a process begun with the poems of *Lord Weary's Castle.* Like all of Lowell's poems since *Life Studies,* these sonnets invoke and challenge the conventions of autobiography; freely fictionalized, they revise the events of his and others' lives with an aesthetic that, like Browning's, corrects lyric enclosure with the felt vicissitudes of history and the endless unraveling of narrative. Poetry for Lowell is never a self-sufficient form of emotional self-expression but a commitment to a language-process, informed by entire worlds of political and social significance, that shapes rather than merely describes experience. He asserts that writing is a way of engaging the entire self, all the senses. "My eyes have seen what my hand did"—the last line of "Dolphin"—derives, Lowell told Seamus Heaney, from what John Heminge and Henry Condell said about Shakespeare: "His mind and hand went together" (Heaney, 25). For Lowell, this conjunction of mind and body represents a bonding of life and art, a reconciliation of aesthetic and social ideals.

The making of poetry is for Lowell an act of public self-unification, linking hand and eye in the process that Marvell describes as "Annihilating all that's made / To a green thought in a green shade," subsuming the world outside of the poem in a meditative wholeness that rather than being characterized by lyric completion remains porous to larger forms of experience. Its wholeness is that of the world, not of the poem itself. Lowell's "illegible bronze," his obscurities, inexactitudes, and scrawl of revisions, becomes legible in *The Dolphin* as in no previous book; before *Day by Day,* this is his most personal and yet most accessible work. *The Dolphin,* though deeply meditative, as Lowell said, offers a public statement not only about his autobiographical situation but also about the power of his lyrical yet social and historical vision. Though this brief discussion is limited to examining poems containing some of the organizing and linking animal metaphors that help unify the sequence, I hope it will illustrate poetic strategies common to the volume as a whole.

"Fishnet," the thirteen-line sonnet that opens the book, argues through tonal shifts and the contrast between abstract and metaphorical language that both Lowell's aesthetic and his life require freshness, variety, and surprise, even at the risk of unpleasant mood swings and the corresponding dislocations of syntax and diction. The poem introduces two figures, fishnet and dolphin, which recur throughout the book as problems of engagement and difference to suggest the uneasy relationship between Lowell's art and his life.

> Any clear thing that blinds us with surprise,
> your wandering silences and bright trouvailles,
> dolphin let loose to catch the flashing fish. . . .
> Poets die adolescents, their beat embalms them,
> the archetypal voices sing offkey:
> the old actor cannot read his friends,
> and nevertheless reads himself aloud,
> genius hums the auditorium dead.
> The line must terminate.
> Yet my heart rises, I know I've gladdened a lifetime
> knotting, undoing a fishnet of tarred rope;
> the net will hang on the wall when the fish are eaten,
> nailed like illegible bronze on the futureless future. (15)

The opening lines embody the central characteristics of Lowell's poetics: contrast, odd association, and the "bent generalization," a kind of paradox that in the "Afterthought" to *Notebook* he attributes to his devotion to "unrealism." (1969, 262). The strangeness of the poem deepens as we read. The opening two lines in generalized, abstract language invoke the question of how the clarity of his beloved's gestures can engender his own befuddlement, and point to the otherness and quiet withdrawal of the beloved. In contrast, the third line characterizes her in a highly compressed, sensual metaphor of insatiable desire. Alan Williamson describes the effect of lines that so abruptly contrast as "heavy pictures [that] won't hang straight" (16), but Lowell has deliberately extended the immense compression and contrast that are among the principles of sonnet construction inherited from the age of Petrarch. This kind of contrast is common in Shakespeare's sonnets, but most poets since, lacking Shakespeare's sure judgment and daring, have tempered the effect.

After allowing his voice to trail off in ellipses, the speaker falls into six lines of depression, complaining that poets die young ("forever immature"), killed by their obsession with art. For Lowell, especially, the "archetypal voices sing offkey." The actor, the pretender, claims that he no longer reads the work of his friends, and yet he is arrogant enough to present himself as a genius. The line, the lineage, ends with death, but "Fishnet," instead of pursuing that line of termination, looks to inspiration as its own reward. Poetry, he concludes, though it cannot confer immortality, has sufficiently ordered his life. After nine despairing lines, Lowell cheers up because he has discovered a metaphor to clarify his achievement. The inspiration that finds a metaphor to represent a lifetime's accomplishment confers a change in tone, a buoyancy that not even the early appearance of his beloved dolphin, an obsessive figure of otherness and satiation, can compel.

Attempting to explicate the metaphor of the dolphin, Christopher Butler argues that Lowell has derived it from Yeats, although Elizabeth Bishop uses it in "The Riverman," and it figures prominently in Christian art, conventionally representing love, swiftness, and diligence. Butler suggests that the dolphin "seems to stand for Lowell himself, for his guiding Muse (who is also Caroline), and as a symbol of rebirth into a new life consistent with Yeats's use of the symbol, particularly in 'News from the Delphic Oracle'" (151). But this sort of symbol-hunting cannot do justice to the complexity of the dolphin, which embodies complex, unspoken, perhaps unspeakable desires in a life-form allied to but distinct from the human. Paradoxically, it represents the impossibility of fully repre-

senting those desires in a single image. When Lowell initially presents the
dolphin it seems to refer as much to the poetic process—suggesting its
unrational but intelligent animal fervor—as to Caroline or to himself. As
a postmodernist poet (as Randall Jarrell called him as early as 1944), Lowell
no longer uses figures the way the symbolist poets did. Rather than simply representing some abstract mass of social or psychological concerns,
the dolphin, although generated by the will to express the inexpressible,
is most vividly itself—an intelligent alien creature that resists human com-
prehension yet is somehow friendly and companionable. As a trope, it
compels the generation of a larger language of otherness, alienation, and
desire. Most immediately, it brings nature into Lowell's urbanized world,
and thus embodies a pure but knowing form of desire. The ambiguous
syntax of the opening lines of "Fishnet" implies that the "clear thing" is
an attribute of the dolphin, that the characteristics of the beloved make
her a dolphin or that the phrases themselves exemplify dolphin qualities,
that the dolphin is a metaphor of the making of metaphor.

"Fishnet" concludes, as it began, with surprise, a shift in mood. The
closure describes an almost unreservedly joyous shift from morbid brood-
ing to a sense of worthy if elusive purpose, which the rest of the book
will carry out. After asserting that the poem cannot grow and change
forever, that not even adolescence is immortal, Lowell envisions the metaphor that embodies his life's work: a fishnet of tarred rope. This fishnet
most particularly refers to the work of this volume, with its interwoven
metaphors, the "pattern of experience" that Stephen Yenser argued this
book lacks—a pattern of associative metaphor based on a lifetime of attempting to incorporate autobiographical perceptions in a language of
vision (308). Unlike the volatile mood swings of human relationships,
the "wandering silences and bright trouvailles," this fishnet is permanent,
an artifact to nail upon the apocalyptic future. Interestingly, Lowell both
makes and disassembles it. The fishnet alludes to all human endeavor,
whether in life or in art; but it most immediately refers to the text of
Lowell's guiding vision. Seemingly contradicting his vatic stance, his insistence that "writing isn't a craft . . . [that] it must come from some deep
impulse, deep inspiration" (1987, 236–37), this fishnet may seem to privilege craft over vision. However, the net actually represents a concept of
the text in the way Roland Barthes distinguishes text from work, as the
experience of language-texture rather than a fixed, static series of indi-

vidual poems. This conception of text promotes the efficacy of a larger vision of language, not of a craftperson's grasp of the mechanics of poem-making. Lowell has not made a variety of fishnets; he has reworked the same one, not in a hopeless quest for perfection but to keep the ideal poem in mind and view.

In the last four lines of the sonnet Lowell subsumes despair in the pleasure of finding an appropriately evocative language. He "sees" the right images through the compression of the imagination, then with unpredictable modifiers ("illegible" and "futureless"), wrings from it a truth that is not an abstract absolute but the concrete embodiment of his aesthetic purpose. His achievement, this poem argues, does not consist of lasting poems but of a lifetime of tinkering—an Emersonian monument to subjective vision rather than to its imperfect formulation in language. He values that vision, which necessarily dies with him and therefore represents his very essence, more than any finished poem. His historical pessimism and his paradoxical faith in the qualified immortality of the visionary artifact, which assures its own but not its maker's survival, circumscribe his poetic ambition, large though it is. Despite the sort of praise characterized by Randall Jarrell's insistence in reference to *Lord Weary's Castle* that some of Lowell's poems "will be read as long as men remember English" (1953a, 209), the speaker sees the future as "futureless," partly because he won't be in it and partly because historical pessimism points to the inevitable self-destruction of the human race. With the death of humanity and language, all bronze would be "illegible" both in form and in inscription, but in this instance the metal will fade because it is merely a figure of speech. After the fish are eaten, who will remember the use of the net? Illegibly it will endure, meaningless in the absence of the man who made it, a puzzle for alien archaeologists.

The poem unfolds from this metaphor, which reverses a declining concept of the role of poetry and opens up a wider vision of human purpose. By affirming the efficacy of the vatic stance, even when embodied in an illegible monument, the metaphor introduces the larger method and purpose of the book. Subjecting both love relationships and artistic ambition to the pressure of metaphor, the poem exemplifies Lowell's attempt to subsume differing languages of references in the single brief lyric. Contrasting abstraction with metaphor, surviving the despair it generates, "Fishnet" invents an image rich enough to reaffirm and illustrate more than one aspect of Lowell's wry vision and demonstrate its power to order inchoate perceptions in tactile language. The making of fiction and the perceiving of one's life offer differing approaches to knowledge. The dolphin in its natural purity and unbridled spirit exemplifies the juxtaposing of mutually exclusive states of being that throughout this book and his career Lowell attempts to yoke together through tropes of visionary skepticism and a vulnerable will to survive.

"Redcliffe Square," the first designated sequence within the longer work, contrasts new landscapes with familiar established ones. In some of its sonnets, as in many earlier Lowell poems, animal life empowers the landscape. Redcliffe Square is in Brompton, a nineteenth-century section of London's West End. In an interview with Ian Hamilton, Lowell said that between the Orkneys and London he "might find a contrast similar to Maine and New York, but the repetition would seem slovenly" (1971, 10–11). "Redcliffe Square," though avoiding any such feeling of déjà vu, carefully exploits such a contrast. Juxtaposing countryside and city sonnets and mixing the language of each setting, Lowell, in two important poems climaxed or capped with animal imagery, synthesizes these disparate landscapes, which he sees as both opposite and complementary, their dramatic and symbolic functions integrated. As he told Hamilton about those other contrasting landscapes, "these were the places I lived in and also symbols, conscious and unavoidable" (1971, 11).

"Oxford," the fourth poem in the group, pairs the sensual and death-haunted landscape of Mexico with England's gentler, understated meadows, then resolves the disparity through complex shifts of imagery, culminating with a mating of dolphins. These nonhuman analogues, in their ideal constancy, contrast with the speaker's shifting, restless attention, which renders four subtle variants in tone among five distinct images.

> We frittered on the long meadow of the Thames,
> our shoes laminated with yellow flower—
> nothing but the soft of the marsh, the moan of cows,
> the rooster-peacock. Before we had arrived,
> rising stars illuminated Oxford—
> the Aztecs knew these stars would fail to rise
> if forbidden the putrifaction of our flesh,
> the victims' viscera laid out like tiles

on fishponds changed to yellow flowers,
the goldfinchnest, the phosphorous of the ocean
blowing ambergris and ambergris,
dolphin kissing dolphin with a smirking smile,
not loving one object and thinking of another.
Our senses want to please us, if we please them. (17)

Lowell does not mean to suggest that pleasing our senses requires reveling in the grisly horror of human sacrifice, indulging the senses in a romantic natural environment, or even giving oneself up to the love-object at hand. Rather, the source of pleasure he envisions is the realization of the will to trope on natural figures and expose the full force of desire, for which not even human sacrifice is a wholly adequate metaphor. In the oblique closure the mating of the dolphins is not only a dramatic climax but the uninhibited embrace of metaphor as the link between perception and desire. The "bent generalization" of the concluding line throws us back into the poem to reconsider and resolve the otherwise disjunctive imagery in terms of the full complexity of the will and the passions, and the difficulty of achieving an expressive wholeness.

The flowering meadow landscape and the gory landscape of Mexico in their vivid contrast suggest the broad range of Lowell's unrepresented desire. To further suggest the difficulty of realizing the appropriate objective correlative one scene is presented in visual terms and the other in the expository language of history. The dolphin figure engages the whole range of language just as the dolphin, an air-breathing creature living in the sea, spans the full range of intelligent life. Vowel sounds in the first three lines imitate the feel of the soft ground, the low cow-voices. In energetic contrast, the *f* sounds of lines six and seven and the mushy syllables of "putrefaction" prepare us for the emphatic consonants of "victims's viscera." By now we are far from Oxford, but the associational leaps from viscera to tiles to fishponds back to yellow flowers to birds' nests to the ocean and finally to the dolphin are justified both aurally and pictorially because they extend a pattern established early in the poem. That is, both meadow and Mexico define themselves in sound as well as image; the *o* of "ponds," "gold," "phosphorous," and "blowing" leads us to the dolphin by aural as well as pictorial associations.

Lowell links poetry to the dolphin as an engendering figure, but identifies his more private desires with the mermaid, a figure of distinct sexual and psychic otherness. Her half-animal, half-godlike form suggests the way he perceives and wants to render the world in poetry, while the dolphin manifests the nexus of his unrealized and unnamed desires. The mermaid, though a figure of otherness and sexual entanglement, is so rich and self-contained a metaphor that Lowell can hardly face its full implications, can hardly contain her unbridled passion in a poem. In the final sonnet of the sequence entitled "Mermaid," Lowell confesses that he lacks the maturity and courage to embrace his metaphor in its full exuberance and plumb the dark of his psyche to bring her into the full light:

> One wondered who would see and date you next,
> and grapple for the danger of your hand.
> Will money drown you? Poverty, though now
> in fashion, debases women as much as wealth.
> You use no scent, dab brow and lash with shoeblack,
> willing to face the world without more face.
> I've searched the rough black ocean for you,
> and saw the turbulence drop dead for you,
> always lovely, even for those who had you,
> Rough Slitherer in your grotto of haphazard.
> I lack manhood to finish the fishing trip.
> Glad to escape beguilement and the storm,
> I thank the ocean that hides the fearful mermaid—
> like God, I almost doubt if you exist. (37)

Inseparable from her seascape, the mermaid is a creature of myth and nature too defiantly phenomenal for the poet to accept with ease. The ambiguous syntax of the last line suggests that Lowell himself may be "like God," who may have forgotten or never known that he had created a creature whose willingness to "face the world without more face" mocks the speaker's reluctance to face her. Primarily an aesthetic phenomenon, a living paradox, the mermaid offers a heady mixture of love and brutality and a vital example of synthesis and complexity reflected in the associative syntax and structure of the poem.

The mermaid is temptress, siren, and aesthetic model; the dolphin, on the other hand, guides by analogy with the natural order, and, because it speaks to and for the elemental self, engages the wholeness of art and life. That it guides by "surprise" indicates Lowell's reliance on contrast, juxtaposition, and association as lyric strategies intended to tap the unconscious. The magnificent concluding sonnet, "Dolphin," surprises by comparing the dolphin, as figure of both Lowell's beloved and of himself as integrated man and poet, to the voice of Phèdre drawing "Racine, the man of craft," through his "maze of iron composition"—an image of poetry vastly differing from the *ars poetica* of tentativeness, flexibility, and ambiguity through which Lowell usually describes his own work.

> My dolphin, you only guide me by surprise,
> forgetful as Racine, the man of craft,
> drawn through his maze of iron composition
> by the incomparable wandering voice of Phèdre.
> When I was troubled in mind, you made for my body
> caught in its hangman's-knot of sinking lines,
> the glassy bowing and scraping of my will. . . .
> I have sat and listened to too many
> words of the collaborating muse,
> and plotted perhaps too freely with my life,
> not avoiding injury to others,
> not avoiding injury to myself—
> to ask compassion . . . this book, half fiction,
> an eelnet made by man for the eel fighting—
> my eyes have seen what my hand did. (78)

The dolphin, mediating between the natural and the human worlds, replaces the muse as a source of inspiration and embodies Lowell's roles as lover and as romantic artist inflamed by the mystery of creation. When he had confused inspiration with passion, his dolphin untangled him from his undirected desires, tangled into a "hangman's knot," the perversion of the fisherman's knots he has spent a lifetime weaving. The "collaborating muse," rejected in favor of the dolphin, instead of boundless animal energy, offered only "too many words." Collaboration, instead of transcendence, offers only compromise. As Lowell's poems often argue, words alone do not make poetry, which requires the full focus of imagination, perception, and desire. He has, he now realizes, damaged himself and others with a commitment to a language that could not fully account for the social disruptions and pain of his desire, but he asks no forgiveness; he took action in full awareness of the consequences for himself and others. Now he responds to the urgency of his emotional situation by fashioning an eelnet to contain the unbridled animal self and knit together his illegible poetry and chaotic life. This eelnet (the "fishnet of tarred rope" of "Fishnet"), enmeshes a lifetime's work in poetry and the totality of a man who has tried to understand himself. The elusive nature of his prey excludes poetry, a product wholly of the human mind (at least until the bonding of art and life occur), as the focus of Lowell's ambition; the eel or fish ensnared by this net, because it is the total embodiment of desire, must remain outside the poem in the natural world of otherness. Though beyond the domesticating power of language, this embodiment of desire functions as the focus of Lowell's ambition. Naming it, however tentatively, as a phallic force from the lower world brings into mutual focus Lowell's poetic ego and the sexual rage to possess another.

By asserting the mutual engagement of mind (perception) and the made object (the poem), the last line of "Dolphin" asserts the banishment of binary opposites in a larger assertion of the power of trope not to transcend but to incorporate disparities. The entire structure of the book builds to this single trope, which may seem overprivileged, but the plot as well as the figurative language points to the reconciliation of incompatibles. Through the annihilating power of his vision, which places metaphor under tremendous pressure, Lowell brings intellect and sensuality, mind and body, self and not-self together in the flexible, containing figure of the net. The net not only can trap dolphin and mermaid, it also enmeshes vision and craft, love and effort, in a single complex weave. The dolphin, in the book's dominant trope of inspiration, has chosen Lowell and has required him to rise in the dark night of his soul and explore the landscape of necessity and desire. There he would learn to plot his life and aesthetic to coincide and mutually illuminate. To argue that he had to couch this adventure in the privileged terms of aesthetic accomplishment confirms that for the poet healing comes through lyric meditation on the complexities of human relationships and the individual's relationship to the world. Telling his story, half fiction, half history, requires an angle of vision that penetrates the barriers between apparent incompatibles and links his autobiographical longings, however inexpressible, with his concretely lyric way of seeing. The aesthetic that discovered the dolphin, and which the figure of the dolphin embodies, assures Lowell's survival for that moment as poet and person. Elliptical in its compression of plot and expansive in the texture of its figuration, *The Dolphin* concludes Lowell's six-year unrhymed-sonnet obsession (1967–73) and tempers the aesthetic disjunction between his historical-autobiographical impulses and his lyric sensibility by demonstrating that literature and life, half fact, half fiction, are merely two equally fruitful sources of desire and the language to express or memorably repress it.

Lowell, Ammons, Ashbery, and Glück

The significance of Lowell's career-long critique of the autobiographical mode of poetry is not universally appreciated. In a pointedly unsympathetic introduction to a collection of essays, Harold Bloom names Lowell's particular contribution as the origination of the trope of vulnerability and the subsequent fostering of the confessional school of poetry, and then argues that, more than ten years after his death, Lowell's influence, due to the numbing effects of this trope, is less than one would have supposed:

> From *Life Studies* (1959) on, Lowell took up his own revisionary version of William Carlos Williams's rhetorical stance as a defense against his own precursors, T.S. Eliot and Allen Tate. This stance, which is in Williams a fiction of nakedness, becomes in Lowell the trope of vulnerability. The trope, once influential and fashionable, has become the mark of a school of poets who now seem writers of period pieces: the "Confessional" school of Anne Sexton, Sylvia Plath, the earlier W.D. Snodgrass, the later work of John Berryman. (1987, 1)

Bloom correctly names the rhetorical figuration that distinguishes much of Lowell's most important poetry from that of his predecessor poets, but discounts this originality by overstating Lowell's indebtedness and struggles with his poetic father figures, underestimating the range of knowledge made available by the trope of vulnerability, and insisting that the influence of Ashbery, for example, now looms much larger than Lowell's. Arguing further and exposing his own vulnerability, Bloom claims that "Elizabeth Bishop is now firmly established as the enduring artist of Lowell's generation, since the canonical sequence of our poetry seems to many among us, myself included, to move from Stevens through Bishop on to James Merrill and John Ashbery, whose extraordinary works of the last decade are a range beyond anything in Lowell or Berryman" (1987, 2). The shallowness of this appeal to a narrowly defined canon seems obvious enough, but the purpose of this essay is not to measure Lowell's status against Ashbery's, Bishop's, or anyone else's. Rather, I wish to demonstrate that the trope of vulnerability, given distinct voice by Lowell, remains a central rhetorical motif in contemporary poetry, and indeed is most alive in the work of some of the best poets now in midcareer, including poets Bloom habitually singles out for praise.

After considering how Lowell constructs this key trope, using as examples two poems from different parts of his career, "Skunk Hour," from *Life Studies,* and "For John Berryman" from *Day by Day,* I will demonstrate how similar rhetorical elements, configured in psycholinguistic narratives of exposure and withdrawal, shape A.R.Ammons's poem "Easter Morning" and John Ashbery's "Sighs and Inhibitions," and will conclude with a brief discussion of Louise Glück's "Snow" to suggest how a younger generation of poets, just entering midcareer and middle age, has begun to build upon Lowell's example.

Critics have commonly described Ammons as a neo-romantic concerned with the interface between the worlds of nature and culture. Bloom calls him a poet of the "Romantic Sublime" (1976, 220), and Robert Pinsky comments that Ammons's poetry makes "a difficult marriage of poetics or epistemology with natural description: the fluid landscape and the poet's repeated definition of his own role in relation to that flux" (1976, 150). The marriage, however, never quite consummates itself, and the trope of vulnerability exposes the rhetorical gap between the recalcitrant parties. Ashbery, on the other hand, has struck most critics (including Bloom) as a direct descendent of Wallace Stevens, whose revision of high romanticism critiques the generalized, composite voice of poetry described by Mary Jacobus as "disembodied sound" (181) and offers a voice that while resisting autobiography makes certain "ghostlier demarcations, keener sounds" available. Bloom places Ashbery, a much-belated romantic, in descent from Emerson, Whitman, and Stevens as a poet of the "American Sublime" (1976, 199). Ashbery is certainly indebted to Stevens and Whitman, but in many of his poems the trope of vulnerability lends an air of self-deprecating irony, a fostering of personal presence different from that found in Stevens. Lowell's example may have helped generate the tension between Ashbery's commitment to Stevens's distanced, philosophical meditative voice and the more personal note of exhaustion and candor that makes Ashbery's poems seem so intimate yet so oblique. I do not claim that Ammons and Ashbery in midcareer fell under the spell of Lowell; but rather that to some extent they have followed the pattern set by Lowell and Berryman of a midcareer crisis that introduces a note of tension and desire that manifests itself in a way well-described by Bloom's term for what he believes is Lowell's meager contribution to American poetry.

Bloom's argument that the trope of vulnerability, "once influential and fashionable, has become the mark of a school of poets who now seem writers of period pieces," a school of confessional poets, suggests that he has taken too seriously a superficial designation from the literary journalism of the early 1960s. Even M.L. Rosenthal, who originated the term "confessional," has repudiated it as obviously inaccurate and sensationalist. Using so vacuous a term limits the discussion to a small group of sometimes rather histrionic poets. This prevents Bloom from appreciating how Lowell's use of this trope has extended the range of the personal lyric by reshaping it to better embrace the psychological conditions of contemporary culture, and how Lowell's project has influenced and partly shaped some of the contemporary poets Bloom most admires.

The trope of vulnerability, as Bloom describes it in Lowell, derives from Williams's "fiction of nakedness," but I would argue that it greatly complicates the earlier poet's relatively simple desire to articulate ordinary domesticity. Trope, in Bloom's terms, is a complicated issue. In "Poetic Crossing: Rhetoric and Psychology" he describes trope as "one of two possibilities—either the will translating itself into a verbal act or figure of *ethos,* or else the will failing to translate itself and so abiding as a figure of pathos" (1988, 161). A trope, he goes on to argue, is "a reader's awareness of a poet's willed error" (162), but his subsequent work with tropes indicates that they can be textually described as if they were a rhetorical strategy—a strategy, Bloom notes, of a "synchronic rhetoric" (162). The important issues are that tropes defend against the tropes of predecessor poets, that they define themselves in terms of the poet's will to escape an influence perceived as threatening, and that they represent intention as a will to signify. Keeping these issues in mind, but proceeding from Bloom's practice as well as his theory, I would define trope as a collective mode of figuration centered in a will or desire articulated as a rhetorical correlative for an anxiety of some kind.

The trope of vulnerability, then, is a body of rhetorical strategies derived from the poet's desire to either expose or conceal a vulnerable state or feeling. In "Skunk Hour," perhaps the poem in which the trope occurs for the first time, the psychological imperative is the fear of madness, and the poet's will to expose that fear propels the poem into confrontation with debased versions of the cultural and natural sublime. The allegory of unnaturalness or debasement of the natural begins with images of senility, class degradation, and homophobia, and concludes with the skunk family, surely one of the lower (yet still recognizable and credible) manifestations of the natural sublime. The trope of vulnerability, bracketed by this material, occurs in the fifth and sixth stanzas in which the speaker exposes the unnaturalness of his situation and his obsessions:

> One dark night,
> my Tudor Ford climbed the hill's skull;
> I watched for love-cars. Lights turned down,
> they lay together, hull to hull,
> where the graveyard shelves on the town. . . .
> My mind's not right.
>
> A car radio bleats,
> "Love, O careless Love. . . ." I hear
> my ill-spirit sob in each blood cell,
> as if my hand were at its throat. . . .
> I myself am hell;
> nobody's here— (1959, 90)

The psychological degradation of the conventional role of the beholder, the allusion to the self-effacement of Satan and Emily Dickinson, and the emotionally simplistic popular song engender a body of reference that links in cultural continuity a problem that is peculiarly the speaker's and to which he openly lays claim. His mind isn't right not only because he has perverted his sexual desires but because he identifies himself as an absence, a positive lack of normal sensibility. The desire to expose his oncoming madness empowers this imagery with a sense of urgency and significance it would not otherwise have. The competing automobiles— the ironically designated Tudor (for two-door) Ford and the love-cars lying "hull to hull"—, the bleating of the popular song, and the sobbing in the blood cells are ignited by the simple claims to insanity and absence. Rather than being merely allegorically descriptive, as the stanzas about the village are, these two stanzas, although their imagery is not especially vivid or startling, seem to plumb the depths of the speaker's psychological being. The exposure of the will to ward off madness by naming it illuminates the beholder by ringing with hell-fire everything he beholds. Internalized, the imagery assumes a metaphorical dimension the first four stanzas lack, a dimension only describable in terms of aporia, a gap between the text and the will that created it. This gap calls attention to the inadequacy of the available rhetorical means and renders each specific figure—the cars, the graveyard, the blood-cells, even the skunks—as what Bloom might call a figure of pathos (1988, 161). The will cannot fully translate into figuration so overpowering a sensation as oncoming madness and has to name it: thus charming away, if the speaker is fortunate, the rush of incoherence that looms ahead. This failure of figuration renders the poem vulnerable to overreading as a poem "about" madness by exposing the poet's vulnerability through the admission of a desire for which he has no objective correlative available. If "Skunk Hour" is confessional, what it confesses is the poet's inadequacy of verbal resources, and this, surely, is the most poignant admission of vulnerability any poet can make.

If the trope of vulnerability in "Skunk Hour" inspirits ordinary imagery with the psychological imperative of warding off madness, that same trope in "For John Berryman" exposes the speaker's inability to compound a rhetorical charm against death. Here the trope refutes nostalgia and reveals the inability of writing to fend off aging and decay:

> Yet really we had the same life,
> the generic one

our generation offered
(*Les Maudits*—the compliment
each American generation
pays itself in passing):
first students, then with our own,
our galaxy of grands maîtres,
our fifties' fellowships
to Paris, Rome and Florence,
veterans of the Cold War not the War—
all the best of life . . .
then daydreaming to drink at six,
waiting for the iced fire,
even the feel of the frosted glass,
like waiting for a girl . . .
if you had waited.
We asked to be obsessed with writing,
and we were. (1977a, 27)

Lowell wrote the poem sometime after Berryman's suicide in 1972 and apostrophized it to his dead friend. This casual use of apostrophe to address not a god or other emblematic figure but a dead friend, along with the disarmingly casual free verse, distinguishes this poem from more traditional elegies. Valorizing the poet's own descent into age and voicing nostalgia—as bald an admission of verbal inadequacy as the blunt statement "My mind's not right"—renders the poem vulnerable to overreading as a sentimental recounting of a friendship; but the failure of obsessive writing to stall the inevitable descent into age demystifies the poem and implies the need for an alternate mode of discourse. The poet's admission of surprise at the end—

To my surprise, John,
I pray *to* not for you,
think of you not myself,
smile and fall asleep.

—exposes his awareness of the aporia between subject and object, a gap to cross not with ordinary verbiage but with a prayer, the actual words of which the poem withholds. Prayer, a mode of discourse this poem does not actually imitate (it doesn't exhort or praise, for example), fills the aporia, and the speaker is able to avoid thinking of himself at least long enough to fall asleep and escape, by extraliterary means, his disarticulating bout of nostalgia. Writing, with which both Berryman and Lowell "asked to be obsessed," sets the terms of this poem. The speaker's awareness of his tendency toward nostalgia and even sentiment generates a psychological imperative to privilege prayer over poetry, the absent but apostrophized other (Berryman) over the self. The trope of vulnerability develops in the tension between poetry and prayer, between a discourse of nostalgia and one of otherness. Prayer requires sharply defined apostrophe and faith to subsume the literary gesture in literalness. Lowell invokes then conquers apostrophe by postulating Berryman as an actual presence and rejects the literariness of his nostalgia. He surprises himself in doing so, and therefore reveals the will to escape nostalgia—which the speaker was not aware of—that underlies the poem. Although, unlike the controlling trope of "Skunk Hour," this is an escape from pathos rather than a concession to it, this does not result in a more adequate figuration but simply in closure. Prayer is not poetry and Lowell does not attempt to present it as such; but he does confound prayer and poetry as means to a common end, which is the reconciliation of the dead and the living. Prayer might be the more adequate means to this end, but it lies outside the poem. This confounding illustrates what Bloom calls the tendency of "all strong poetry to misread all language that is not poetry" (1988, 162). Lowell's misreading of prayer occurs in a narrative uncertainty between the poem and the prayer, but it is part of the rhetorical structure of this poem's trope of vulnerability.

In Ammons's "Easter Morning" the psychological imperative shaping the trope of vulnerability is the poet's will to voice his doubtful other, the self that did not develop. Although this self had at one time a palpable form—a brother who died, apparently in an accident, when very young—that other has been absorbed into the psyche of the speaker so that he cannot clearly distinguish himself from the child who died. That dead brother has become an alternate version of himself, a life he failed to lead. Because this self did not develop it lacks a footing in the world that would offer it imagery sufficient to embody its emotional needs. Consequently, the poet has to name it as something inside of him, "like a pregnancy," and paradoxically, if authentically, like someone already dead:

> I have a life that did not become,
> that turned aside and stopped,
> astonished:
> I hold it in me like a pregnancy or
> as on my lap a child
> not to grow or grow old but dwell on
>
> it is to his grave I most
> frequently return and return
> to ask what is wrong, what was
> wrong, to see it all by
> the light of a different necessity (19)

This is as confessional as anything in Lowell, and courts the pathos of inarticulation by its seeming refusal to find adequate or consistent imagery and admit the direct expression of the will. However, with a shift in syntax and cadence the poem suffers through a nostalgic visit to the poet's childhood home, then argues that the child in him that "could not become" failed to develop because he refused the language of nostalgia, memory, and change:

> the child in me that could not become
> was not ready for others to go,
> to go on into changes, blessings and
> horrors, but stands there by the road
> where the mishap occurred, crying out for
> help, come and fix this or we
> can't get by, but the great ones who
> were to return, they could not or did
> not hear and went on in a flurry

The price is "bitter incompletions," and neither the child who never grew up nor the child who became a man escapes their emotional weight.

Now the poem literalizes the psychological inner child as a "little brother who died," explaining in narrative rather than lyric terms the relationship between the speaking and the regretted selves. But tonally colored by the trope of vulnerability, this poem continues not as an elegy for a dead brother but as a lyric encounter with a failure of will, a failure of the speaker to realize his own not his brother's possibilities:

> it is my place where
> I must stand and fail,
> calling attention with tears
> to the branches not lofting
> boughs into space, to the barren
> air that holds the world that was my world

Empowered with a sense of natural presence unmatched by other contemporary poets, Ammons escapes pathos by discovering in the drama of "two great birds" allegorical imagery graceful and persuasive enough to resolve the aporia between articulate self and inarticulate other. However, even after describing in detail the movements and relationship of the birds, the poet is forced to acknowledge that the psychological imperative that generated this poem resists the objective correlative, finding it too seamless and self-privileged, and injects an insistent note of banality to remind us that the psyche finds all language insufficient to atone for the will to despair:

> it was a sight of bountiful
> majesty and integrity: the having
> patterns and routes, breaking
> from them to explore other patterns or
> better ways to routes

The plain inadequacy of "bountiful / majesty and integrity" refutes the lyric temptation to impose an illusion of articulation on the trope of vulnerability that controls this poem. Ammons consciously and conscientiously retains the possibility of pathos and refuses the easier comfort of a lyric solution to a psychological unease. The willed error courted here is the heresy of violating culture with nature, concealing human disorder beneath a veneer of natural process. Ammons can court and then reject this error because he articulates the play of natural forms with such precision that he easily convinces us of the possibility of accepting a lyrical-allegorical closure to an internal, extraliterary problem. But he values his vulnerability as much as he values nature; in fact, one relationship the poem toys with would render natural and human vulnerability as equal. But Ammons resists this, too, in part because the human and bird worlds are not really equal. The birds occupy a larger and older world because they have no history, personal or otherwise. They are truly in their world, while the speaker resides most truly in himself. Ammons resists violating this dichotomy, and therefore places psychological over poetic decorum.

Ashbery differs from either Lowell or Ammons in having made vulnerability the overt subject of much of his poetry. However, having done so does not inoculate his work against the pathos, aporia, and willed error that characterize the trope. His early work seemed somewhat Auden-like in its relative lack of psycho-semantic aporia and its resistance to psychological imperatives of the kind that court inarticulation. However, from Stevens he learned how the undercurrents of passion disarticulate allegory; and whether with the example of Lowell or simply with the onset of poetic maturity, his work from *The Double Dream of Spring* to the present day often embraces the trope of vulnerability with the fervor of religious conversion. The consequent failure of allegory, deliberately courted, gives his poetry a characteristic air of nostalgia for the inarticulate.

The psychological imperative of "Sighs and Inhibitions" is the will to resist the orderly compromise that makes ordinary life possible but exacts the price of conformity and social responsibility. The poem's trope of vulnerability shapes itself about imagery of articulation ("Some angle or hinge / Bulkier than stone and more resilient than the ideas / That have helped to put it across") and violence ("throwing a small rock / At some kid I hated"), two perfectly rational responses to order imposed by impersonal circumstance. The early sections of the poem, which speak themselves in the third person ("one invests the compromise / Quite early") or first-person plural ("so that it is it, not we, / That is our lives") court yet resist the trope of vulnerability. But the last two sections unfold the trope and explicate the psychological inarticulation that is the generating motive of the poem. Here Ashbery relinquishes the impersonality of the third-person and first-person plural and exposes the pathos of the underlying will:

> I remember in the schoolyard throwing a small rock
> At some kid I hated, and then, when the blood began
> To ooze definitively, trying to hug the teacher,
> The boy, the world, into ignoring what I'd done,
> To lie and thus escape through a simple
> Canceling, not a confession, to wipe the slate clean
> So as to inhabit another world in which
> I bore no responsibility for my acts: life
> As a clear, living dream.
>
> And I have not been spared this
> Dreadful state of affairs, no one has, so that
> When we think we think, or turn over in our sleep,
> Someone else's business is boldly attached to this,
> And there is no time for a reckoning.
> The carpet never stretches quite far enough,
> There is always a footfall on the stair. (1987, 51–52)

The last two lines turn the poem from pathos by finding metaphor sufficient to embody the very inadequacy of language to stretch "quite far enough" to cover one's psychological imperatives, so the footfall on the stair uncomfortably resounds in the exposed psyche. However, the poet, to maintain the open stance of vulnerability, confesses to having attempted to avoid confessing, and in doing so exposes the ignorance the will would impose on the child and the poet.

The error here is to have believed, however momentarily, that "canceling" can undo the requirement of "confession," that a metaphorical act (hugging the boy, the teacher, the world) can undo the crime of resistance to the conformity the world demands. There is no escaping the "confession" that risks exposing the will to the possibility of misreading. The trope of vulnerability here consists of the language that despite its clumsy inarticulateness we actually have to use—not one's semi-mythic first language (like Ammons's early lost self) but a "somehow foreign" one,

> this other
> Block-letter language we must carry (and it
> Grows heavier), and place around to form the words
> No one is going to understand, let alone believe,
> And these account for our day, today.

The error courted by the trope of vulnerability in this poem is the error of being understood. Ashbery well knows that no language actually reveals the will in its primal innocence, but the language of the last two sections of the poem runs the risk of seeming to do so, and therefore embodies the vulnerability the poet most fears.

The poetry of confession, Ashbery suggests, reveals the attempt to conceal or cancel our most private expression, our rock throwing, our attempts to escape a language of socialization. For Lowell, too, in "Skunk Hour" inadequate socialization resists a language sufficient to its psychological imperative and he is forced to "confess" in a language that in its very inadequacy renders the speaker vulnerable to misreading. Far from being an outmoded form of discourse, the poetry of confession is the poetry that most courageously skirts the boundaries of articulation, the poetry best prepared to accept the consequences of misreading. The trope of vulnerability organizes the rhetoric of inarticulation as a poetic strategy that points simultaneously to the psychological inadequacy of language and to the rhetorical cunning of verse in accommodating the interface of socialized and unsocialized selves. Ammons in "Easter Morning" expresses the role of verse as a stance, a point from which to behold one's divergent selves in mutual inarticulation:

> though the incompletions
> (& completions) burn out
> standing in the flash high-burn
> momentary structure of ash, still it
> is a picture-book, letter-perfect
> Easter morning: I have been for a
> walk: the wind is tranquil: the brook

works without flashing in an abundant
tranquility

Maintaining one's vulnerability is a way of resisting complete absorption by the social world. It requires resisting the closure of "abundant tranquility"; it requires a distrust of language that too well correlates with the object. With this distrust Lowell most clearly broke with Tate's understanding of Eliot and embraced aspects of high modernism the New Critics hadn't acknowledged. The lesson Lowell derives from his sense of the inadequacy of language—a lesson he could have learned from *Four Quartets* as well as from Mallarmé—is not one of cringing self-obsession but, as Ashbery has learned it, of confession as a way to keep language and the psyche open to each other's imperatives. The poets of the generation following him have learned that lesson well, and the poets of the generation now entering full maturity have begun to show signs of embracing the trope of vulnerability as a means of opening themselves to psychological imperatives for which no metaphors present themselves. Glück's poem "Snow," from *Ararat,* demonstrates the continued appeal and vitality of the trope of vulnerability:

> Late December: my father and I
> are going to New York, to the circus.
> He holds me
> on his shoulders in the bitter wind:
> scraps of white paper
> blow over the railroad ties.
>
> My father liked
> to stand like this, to hold me
> so he couldn't see me.
> I remember
> staring straight ahead
> into the world my father saw;
> I was learning
> to absorb its emptiness,
> the heavy snow
> not falling, whirling around us. (1990, 58)

To not only learn about otherness and absence but to take it into oneself is to escape the grip of the father and face extinction on one's own. The death of the father, a subject in other poems in *Ararat,* is elided from this poem; the trope of vulnerability exposes the gap between what is admissible—grief for the loss of a parent—and what is not: the desire to die. The grief is not available since the death hasn't occurred, but the child has already learned the fear of absence and has generated the will to embrace it. The aporia here is psychologically mandated, and conceals the desire to invoke death as the actual subject and source of desire. The will to express the simultaneous appeal and horror of erasure shapes not only this poem but much of the book.

Glück's plaintive, evasive, and revelatory language echoes Lowell's rejection of his own metaphorically armored early poems and acceptance of the plain speech of the psychological imperative that gave vent to his fear of madness. Glück exposes her fear of emptiness at the risk of pathos because, like Ammons and Ashbery, she values her vulnerability not only as a fact of her life but also as an opening into a larger sense of language, in which the will participates both as a socialized articulateness and as the elided voice of the inarticulate imperative driving it. The expansion of the poet's opportunity to give voice to unsocialized psychic needs is Lowell's legacy, a much greater and more vital one than Bloom seems to realize. The rhetorical stances assumed by Lowell at various points in his career, especially those that challenge and expand the role of the first-person speaker, remain important resources for contemporary and future poets.

Epilogue

Meditation and Impersonality in Contemporary Poetry

Most of the poetry discussed in this book is neither narrative nor dramatic but lyric or meditative or dramatic monologue. From Aristotle to the romantics, lyric was the weaker stepsister of epic and drama. In the romantic period, however, the challenge of the dramatic monologue and what M.H. Abrams has called the "greater Romantic lyric" broadened the range of the brief poem and increased its ability to argue in imagery, to shape a compelling meditation around the dialectic of metaphor, and to confront and embrace history. Critical studies by Herbert Tucker, Cynthia Chase, Loy D. Martin, and others alert to the dialogic paradigm at the heart of discourse have revealed the complexity of characteristic lyric tropes like apostrophe and prosopopoeia, and have demonstrated that under the general genre and categories of lyric and monologue enormously complex rhetorical strategies are operating. The voices of these poems now seem far more problematic than has previously been assumed. This flexibility, demonstrated by romantic and modernist poets, has made "lyric" synonymous with "poetry" to the modern or contemporary reader, while the old identification with song seems decidedly outdated; but "monologue" might better describe most modern and contemporary poetry, since the descent from Browning's and Tennyson's dramatic monologue, by way of Pound, Eliot, and Stevens, is well documented in studies of these poets as individuals and in various groupings.

We live in an era of mixed genres. From the functional view, the novel and the epic merge rather disconcertingly in our culture, so that our historicizing and our larger mythologizing occur most often in the stolid cadences of prose. Drama, usually consigned in our time to an amorphous naturalism, has relinquished the grandeur and ambition of classical and Elizabethan tragedy and has focused on the small, distinct gesture, preferring to render the absurdity of action rather than its enabling power. The lyric, modified by the tendency toward monologue, has survived this realignment of genres, but not without strain and obfuscation and a consequent withdrawal from the more communal, historical voice of the dramatic monologue to the faintly solipsistic voice of the interior monologue.

To conclude this study I will attempt to characterize the strains of meditation (the dominant mode of the short poem since Wordsworth, Tennyson, and Browning) and impersonality (the attitude toward the reader of the solitary and self-confined romantic-modernist lyric) as issues of voice, and will suggest a few of the ways contemporary poets have attempted to deal with them. One way is by embracing the isolated and isolating meditation (John Ashbery), another is by manipulating the traditional pronominal I-you (Louise Glück), and a third is by lowering the voice and register of diction and accepting the consequent lowering of readers' (and speakers') emotional and dramatic expectations (Robert Pinsky). These younger poets are not abandoning the meditative poem to return to the truly dialectic I-you poem; rather, in the aftermath of Williams, Pound, and Stevens they are attempting to retain the heavy reliance on imagery of the romantic meditative poem and find some way to more immediately and familiarly engage the reader by opening the voice of the poem into something more gregarious than the solitary act of meditation. I will briefly consider the broader issues in the rise of the romantic-modernist lyric and later turn to these three examples of the contemporary poet's struggle to consolidate the gains of the meditative poem by either decisively rejecting or attempting to reclaim, in some modified form, the more communal voice of the pronominal I-you poems of classical and Renaissance lyric.

From World to Self

The brief poem, which we call the lyric for lack of a more satisfactory term, has decisively shifted its focus from world to self, as every literary historian since Hazlitt has noticed. Though the dramatic monologue finds another way to embrace history, it is a distinctly subjective genre, too psychological to encourage the kind of social allegory found in *The*

Faerie Queen or *Arcadia*. It has replaced assertion with meditation, and has substituted the contemplation of imagery, with a consequent interest in self-reflexivity, for the mediation between philosophy and history that Sidney claimed as the poet's privilege—a privilege available not only to *Lear* and *The Faerie Queen* but also to the sonnets of Daniel and Drayton.

The meditative voice, like the pronominal I-you voice, has always been available to poets of any era. A meditative poem, as Louis Martz remarks in speaking of the seventeenth-century religious lyric, is one in which "the soul or mind engages in acts of interior dramatization" (xvii). I would amend this, in regard to the romantic and modernist meditative poem, by substituting "voice" for "soul or mind." However, the secular meditative poem of the romantics clearly descends from the religious one, which Martz traces back to that same Augustinian strain of piety in which Perry Miller finds the roots of radical English Protestantism. Other literary historians have argued that this radical Protestantism directly inspirits the romantic insistence on the secular authority of individual experience, which gives rise to the voice of meditation as we find it in Wordsworth and even in Whitman. To trace this evolution is beyond the scope of this essay. I want, however, to note that neither romantic nor modernist, neither Wordsworth nor Stevens invented the meditative lyric, that as much as the I-you poem it is a part of literary history, and that in romanticism and modernism we find a shift of emphasis, not a wholesale invention of entirely new genres. This shift in the secular lyric away from the dramatic to the interior monologue seems one toward solipsism as a necessary poetic stance, a shift in focus I have already defined as one from world to self.

The irony of this shift from world to self is a consequent impersonality that is the result of the abandonment of the lyric's traditional I-you dialectic. The more self-centered the voice the more evident the mode of what Keats labeled the "egoistical sublime," the more inaccessible to the reader and, consequently, however more personal from the speaker's point of view, the more impersonal from the reader's. The work of Wallace Stevens most clearly illustrates this shift, but even the verse of the mislabeled confessional poets seems cool and remote compared to the intimate implication of dialectic in Shakespeare's sonnets. Lowell's "Father's Bedroom" seems as calmly isolated as a museum piece in its reliance on imagery to engender an elegiac nostalgia adequate to its occasion:

In my Father's bedroom:
blue threads as thin
as pen-writing on the bedspread,
blue dots on the curtains,
a blue kimono,
Chinese sandals with blue plush straps.
The broad-planked floor
had a sandpapered neatness.
The clear glass bed-lamp
with a white doily shade
was still raised a few
inches by resting on volume two
of Lafcadio Hearn's
Glimpses of Unfamiliar Japan.
Its warped olive cover
was punished like a rhinoceros hide.
In the flyleaf:
"Robbie from Mother."
Years later in the same hand:
"This book has had hard usage
on the Yangtze River, China.
It was left under an open
porthole in a storm." (1959, 75)

Lowell relies on the richness of description to compensate for this poem's personal—even private—mode of rhetoric, one that refuses to disclose the speaker's emotions but attempts, instead, to generate a roughly corresponding elegiac nostalgia in the reader. Almost solely by appealing to our physical senses he has attempted to make his father's bedroom mean to us something analogous to what it means to him; and to a great extent he succeeds. However, the voice of the poem actually works against that emotional parallelism, since it is the voice of someone who is so absorbed with the unspecified fact of his father's death and with the meager but palpable historical record of his father's life, so detached from the possibility of human community (in the sense of one person plainly speaking to another) that it completes, perhaps inadvertently, the lyric's small world with neither thought of nor room for the inclusion of even one other breathing if fictive person. The poem speaks to no one except the speaker, and he has nothing to say to us, since only honest acknowledgment of his emotional state would suffice, and that would violate his aesthetic. It is a solitary musing and a beautiful one. We have to enter the poem by way of that beauty, by way of the exactness and plenitude of description, not by the more direct route of the speaker's emotion, which would require a more communally directed expression, a sense of an audience, which the meditative lyric or interior monologue does not usually provide, and which the late modernist aesthetic of Lowell, at the time this poem was written, had not yet embraced.

Catullus, on the other hand, with the dynamic of the implied dialectic, engenders a rhetorical urgency that the reader, by virtue of relationship to the text and to the fiction of the I–you construct, is forced to share:

> Alfene, you're both ungrateful and untrue.
> Cruel fellow, incapable of caring
> for your honorary brother, you'd trick me,
> then guiltless, withdraw? Unimpressed
> by the gods' disdain for treachery
> and hypocrisy you'd abandon me
> to my grief? What should I do? Where
> should I place my trust? You baited me
> into friendship; then, dear enemy,
> said, "Love me, without restraint." Now
> you sell me out and leave me dangling,
> and scatter your words and deeds
> on the wind. Whether you've forgotten,
> the gods haven't—nor does honor ignore
> falseheartedness. This isn't over yet.
> (Translated by William Doreski)

Lowell's poem conforms to the convention of the overheard meditation limited by its fictional lack of audience; Catullus's conforms to the convention of the overheard conversation. Clearly the latter is more open to the reader, for two reasons. First, the act of reading more clearly resembles conversation in its dynamic than it does meditation, since read-

ing occurs between two parties, reader and text, while meditation is a
solitary, self-referential act. Second, conversation is a dynamic that conforms to our daily fiction of otherness, our faith that the world, despite
Bishop Berkeley, actually exists and that we enjoy communion with others as a confirmation of our own existence. Lowell's poem denies us this
dynamic; Catullus's poem confirms it.

The disappearance of this conversational fiction is not absolute.
Modern and contemporary poets have tried various strategies to revive it,
or some comparable rhetorical dynamic, to counter the flat affect of the
meditative voice and the impersonality of the solitary musing. In recent
years the second-person poem has enjoyed a vogue, but this strategy only
renders half of the fiction of dialectic, leaving the first person dangling
somewhere in the reader's freewheeling imagination. A superior poem in
this manner is Alan Dugan's "On an East Wind from the Wars":

> The wind came in for several thousand miles all night
> and changed the close lie of your hair this morning.
> > It
> has brought well-travelled sea-birds who forget
> their passage, singing. Old songs from the old
> battle- and burial-grounds seem new in new lands.
> They have to do with spring as new in seeming as
> the old air idling in your hair in fact. So new,
> so ignorant of any weather not your own,
> you like it, breathing in a wind that swept
> the battlefields of their worst smells, and took the
> > dead
> unburied to the potter's field of air. For miles
> they sweetened on the sea-spray, the foul washed off,
> and what is left is spring to you, love, sweet,
> the salt blown past your shoulder luckily. No
> wonder your laugh rings like a chisel as it cuts
> your children's new names in the tombstone of the air. (2)

Yet this, too, as an antidote to modernist impersonality and meditation's
neutral gray is unsatisfactory. We have an implied dialectic, but the speaker's
role remains unclear. Does the addressed person really require the speaker

to explain—to meditate upon—his or her situation in this way? The fiction is unconvincing because we cannot understand why the poem requires the second person. Except for the solitary phrase "lover, sweet" the poem, as far as its rhetorical dynamic is concerned, would seem much the same if written in the first person. A far more convincing use of the second person, and one that clearly shows how the second person works as half of the I-you paradigm, is Shakespeare's sonnet 128:

> How oft, when thou, my music, music play'st
> Upon that blessed wood whose motion sounds
> With thy sweet fingers, when thou gently sway'st
> The wiry concord that mine ear confounds,
> Do I envy those jacks that nimble leap
> To kiss the tender inward of thy hand,
> Whilst my poor lips, which should that harvest reap,
> At the wood's boldness by thee blushing stand!
> To be so tickled, they would change their state
> And situation with those dancing chips
> O'er whom thy fingers walk with gentle gait,
> Making dead wood more blest than living lips.
>   Since saucy jacks so happy are in this,
>   Give them thy fingers, me thy lips to kiss.

Here the interplay of first-person speaker and addressed second person renders a dramatically satisfying fiction of love play overheard, a love play in which the reader finds confirmed his or her own conviction that a text is something that happens between two parties, whether lover and beloved or reader and printed page.

Yet the very struggle to deal with impersonality is responsible for much of the rhetorical power of the best poetry from Wordsworth and Keats to the present. W.R. Johnson bemoans Wordsworth's alleged perversion of his brief 1798 "Prelude," "very possibly the freshest, the greatest lyric poem in the language," into a poem "murdered" by "insipid philosophizing and destructive moralism and demented religiosity" (7). He argues that "the destruction of the pronominal form (Wordsworth no longer addressing his poem to Coleridge, as if to thee alone) is symptomatic of the larger ruin of this poem's initial transparencies and unique exultations" (7–8). I have reservations about his utter dismissal of the longer *Prelude,* but I agree with his implication that the loss of the pronominal I-you dynamic is a synecdoche of larger changes in the lyric's rhetoric and intention as it moves toward first the dramatic then the interior monologue. To attribute the difficulties of the modern poem solely to the loss of the I-you dialectic would be as obtuse as to credit its pleasures to its impersonality. The new dynamic is a function of the tension between impersonality and the fiction of self-revelation; if the reader has to adopt a new stance to read this poem, it is one we can learn by reading "To Autumn" as well as *The Waste Land* and "Hibernaculum."

"To Autumn," in fact, provides an especially vibrant test case. The poem, because of or despite its sustained apostrophe, seems modernist and impersonal; addressed to a goddess by a faceless speaker, it avoids the I-you dynamic, and though it is a second-person poem it remains wholly meditative in rhetoric and intent. No critic, no student, no one I know of considers this poem a failure (though some, like Allen Tate, have wondered if it is really about anything). It succeeds because while it refuses the reader the easy foothold of the pronominal I-you poem, substituting the apostrophe, an inherently less satisfactory mode of address, its sweep of imagery is so inclusive and so thoroughly engages the various senses of the imagination that the reader enters the text as though it were a place rather than a human situation, a place composed not solely of landscape but of the process of becoming so that we instinctively identify with our own growth and ongoing state of being in the world.

Each stanza offers a different kind of invitation into the spatial world of the poem's becoming. The second stanza invites us into that place by encouraging us to visualize the resident goddess:

> Who hath not seen thee oft amid thy store?
>   Sometimes whoever seeks abroad may find
> Thee sitting careless on a granary floor,
>   Thy hair soft-lifted by the winnowing wind;

but the purposeful reader is already there, fully alerted to this poem's potential for confirming our existence by the first stanza's exposition of the sensuous possibilities of this rhetorical dynamic:

Season of mists and mellow fruitfulness,
   Close bosom-friend of the maturing sun;
Conspiring with him how to load and bless
   With fruit the vines that round the thatch-eves run;
To bend with apples the moss'd cottage-trees,
   And fill all fruit with ripeness to the core;
     To swell the gourd, and plump the hazel shells
   With a sweet kernel; to set budding more,
And still more, later flowers for the bees,
Until they think warm days will never cease,
     For summer has o'er brimmed their clammy cells.

By the time Keats asks Autumn "Where are the songs of spring?" he has already convinced us that his song, autumn's song, is our song, and the music of autumn, which he proceeds to unfold in the most perfect lines in English poetry, more than adequately compensates for the loss of the easier dynamic of human contact. The dialogue of the senses engendered by this poem is more powerfully self-confirmatory than the I-you fiction of interchange:

While barred clouds bloom the soft-dying day,
   And touch the stubble-plains with rosy hue;
Then in a wailful choir the small gnats mourn
   Among the river sallows, borne aloft
     Or sinking as the light wind lives or dies;
And full-grown lambs bleat from hilly bourn;
   Hedge-crickets sing; and now with treble soft
   The red-breast whistles from a garden-croft;
     And gathering swallows twitter in the skies.

"To Autumn" teaches us how to argue in images, and demonstrates that the pronominal mode is only one variety of the argument of lyric, an argument between the fiction of being and the fact of form, with rhetoric as the mediator of the argument.

    William Carlos Williams, among the most adventuresome of modern American poets, learned this method of argument from Keats, along with a good deal of crude surface texture that he quickly shed. Williams tried many fictional voices, but in the end his greatest achievement may have been to revitalize the old pronominal mode in the context of an argument of thoroughly domestic imagery, clearly seen in the brief poem "This Is Just to Say":

> I have eaten
> the plums
> that were in
> the icebox
>
> and which
> you were probably
> saving
> for breakfast
>
> Forgive me
> they were delicious
> so sweet
> and so cold (1986, 372)

The simple fiction of the note left to explain a minor household matter here embodies all the rhetorical possibilities of human interaction in a world of objects. The addressed person isn't actually present: nor, any longer, are the plums. The poem itself will substitute for both plums and speaker, as the actual note would, and indeed it offers this substitution in just the same way for both the reader and the actual if fictional second person. This is a paradigm of the lyric, the imitation of a speech act not merely overheard but appropriated by the reader, for whom those plums are as sweet and cold as for the addressed person and as nonexistent. The very shape of the poem invites participation by providing an accessible surface, breaking syntax into units as digestible as the plums.

Ashbery, Glück, Pinsky

Younger poets have wrestled with the problems and possibilities of lyric impersonality in more ways than I can describe here. But some characteristic examples will suggest that while no easy substitution for the I–you dynamic is available, the use of other voices, other pronominal strategies, may extend the short poem into new areas and may open new ways of seeing ourselves in our recalcitrant culture. In order, the aspects of the problem of voice in contemporary poetry I want to take up here are as follows:

> (1) The problem of the closed narration, in which experience excludes, rather than appeals to, the reader. (What, then, does the poem ask of the reader?)

> (2) The problem of representing an addressed other. (Need that person be part of the actual fictive occurrence of the poem? What happens when the person is merely postulated, so that no true dialectic is possible? How does this resemble the poem of apostrophe, like Keats's?)

> (3) The problem of authenticity. (What happens when the poem is pitched so low that it seems to make no earnest intellectual or emotional demand?)

Many more problems, perhaps as many problems as poems, come to mind, but these examples may indicate the diversity as well as the complexity that follows the divergence from relatively simple pronominal dialectic, on the one hand, and relatively straightforward meditation, on the other.

Ashbery's poems often seem to rely on the I–you convention, but by eliding key information redirect us from the dynamic of verbal intercourse to the afterglow of muted feeling. As we read further into the poem we realize that this speaker has reordered the meditative voice to address himself, self-consciously invoking a reflexivity that excludes the reader more decisively than the solitary I of the ordinary meditative lyric does. "Destiny Waltz," a typical poem in this vein, opens by appealing to a vague idea of human community, then turns inward with the line "Older faces than yours," which the alert reader knows is self-referential on the part of the speaker, and which completes the I–you paradigm by claiming for the meditating self, the fictive speaker, both halves of the pronominal dynamic:

Everyone has some work to be done
And after that they may have some fun.
Which sometimes leads to distraction.
Older faces than yours

Have been whirled away on heaven
Knows what wind like painted leaves in autumn.
Seriousness doesn't help either:
Just when you get on it it slips its tether,
Laughing, runs happily away.

It is a question of forbearance among the days.
Ask, but not too often: that way most ways
Of leading up to the truth will approach you
Timidly at first, wanting to get to know you
Before wandering away on other paths
Leading out of your meanwhile safe precinct.
Your feet know what they're doing.

And if later in the year some true fear,
A real demon comes to be installed
In the sang-froid of not doing anything,
The shoe is on the other foot
This time,
Just this one time.

Romance removes so much of this
Yet staying behind while it does so
Is no way to agitate
To break the year's commotion where it loomed
Sharpest and most full. It's a trance. (1984, 60)

Like the Dugan poem considered earlier, this seems to beg the question of why it invokes the second person. In this instance the poem's
ostensible argument, that destiny keeps its own counsel and cannot be
forced, is an experiential argument not a philosophical one, and seals the
closed circle of meditation against the intrusion of the alternate if equally

undescribed experience of the reader. It is this resolute exclusion of the reader that makes reading Ashbery a beguiling but often frustrating experience. The originality of his poetry is its utter refusal of the universal, its unwillingness to allow the reader to mistake himself or herself for the self as text, a mistake the average lyric in one way or another encourages. But teasing us momentarily with the ease of entry characteristic of the I-you fiction—a speaker who will not even surrender the context of meditation but only the rhetoric peculiar to the instance—Ashbery, to a greater degree than even his modernist predecessors, insists on the inviolable autonomy of the lyric-as-meditation.

More conventional in its use of the pronominal I-you (and its reliance on "we" to assure the reader that this is a community of at least two, rather than a self-reflexive construct), yet striking for the ambiguity of the speaker's approach to the fictive other, is Glück's "Gretel in Darkness." Though this poem has a clearly fictional speaker, it is as confiding and apparently as intimate in its appeal as an ordinary first-person lyricism and in that way characterizes contemporary dramatic monologues, especially those with allegorical ambitions:

> This is the world we wanted.
> All who would have seen us dead
> are dead. I hear the witch's cry
> break in the moonlight through a sheet
> of sugar: God rewards.
> Her tongue shrivels into gas. . . .
>
>   Now, far from women's arms
> and memory of women, in our father's hut
> we sleep, are never hungry.
> Why do I not forget?
> My father bars the door, bars harm
> from this house, and it is years.
>
> No one remembers. Even you, my brother,
> summer afternoons you look at me as though
> you meant to leave,
> as though it never happened.

But I killed for you. I see armed firs,
the spires of that gleaming kiln—

Nights I turn to you to hold me
but you are not there.
Am I alone? Spies
hiss in the stillness, Hansel,
we are there still and it is real, real,
that black forest and the fire in earnest. (1975, 5)

Through its first three sections this poem takes pains to establish the particulars of the I-you relationship (Gretel and her brother Hansel, years after their fabled adventure), then in the last section disavows the actual presence of Hansel in favor of the speaker's knowledge that she is speaking to no one, or rather to a fictive brother, not the one she may actually have but an epistolary reconstruction. This raises the issue of what the fictive presence of the second person means in lyric terms, but Glück's speaker is able to assert only that what once was still is, and only that historical—not actual, even in fictional terms—presence is "real, real." This presence is not a fact of human kinship, it is not Hansel invoked by the comforting fiction of the poem: rather it is the bald landscape of their empowering myth of childhood, "that black forest and the fire in earnest." The reader is privy to a dialectic in which not only the question of presence but the very terms of memory give way to a bleak absence that only a hostile natural world, the ultimate otherness, can fill.

My third example, a poem by Pinsky, is what Jonathan Holden, borrowing from Coleridge and Wordsworth, has called a "conversation poem," one in which the mimesis of conversation precludes most of the more formal aspects of poetic decorum, including nearly all of the sonic and rhetorical devices that so decisively empower "To Autumn." The point is to disarm the reader, to ease entry into the poem by allowing the reader to ask whether this is in fact a poem, to lower expectations and thus refuse the paradigm of ambiguity, allusion, dissemination, and intertextuality in which modernism, New Criticism, and deconstruction have taught us to expect to find poetry armored. Whether this strategy of depoeticizing is self-defeating, whether in fact the extreme lowering of registers of diction precludes the intensity of experience we associate with the reading of a poem, remains to be decided.

Pinsky's "Long Branch, New Jersey" is poignantly colloquial, casual, and as dependent on the I-you dialectic as Catullus's poem is, but without the urgency:

> Everything is regional,
> And this is where I was born, dear,
> And conceived,
> And first moved to tears,
> And last irritated to the same point.
>
> It is bounded on three sides by similar places
> And on one side by vast, uncouth houses
> A glum boardwalk and,
> As we say, The Beach.
>
> I stand here now
> At the corner of Third Avenue and Broadway
> Waiting for you to come by in a car,
> And count the red carlights
> That rush through a fine rain
> To where Broadway's two branches—North
> Broadway and South Broadway—both reach
> To the trite, salt, welcoming ocean. (1975, 48)

For me, the issue is not, as Holden would have it, the "authority of the speaking voice" (33), but the authenticity of the act of reading this poem: that is, its legitimacy and potency as an experience between reader and text. The reader enters the poem easily, the I-you dialectic clearly delineated, the setting clear and purposeful, and the emotional context—the boundaries of the speaker's emotion—surveyed in the first verse paragraph. The second section similarly surveys the physical boundaries that correspond to the speaker's emotional boundaries, and the third suggests that the speaker expects the second person, the addressed other, to enter this poem from a different world, the world of cars and lights. This person in entering this poem would presumably break the powerful spell of familiarity in which even the ocean is "trite," though it is also "salt" and

"welcoming" and is the only aspect of the landscape that is conventionally metaphorical.

Easily entered, like a Williams I-you poem, "Long Branch, New
Jersey" lacks the rhetorical urgency of Williams's best poems. The problem is that the speaker relies on someone else—ostensibly the addressed
other person, but actually the reader—to complete the poem by breaking
through the boundaries of a world—a poem—where "everything is re-
gional." The speaker is exhausted by her (?) landscape, which she renders
with mild irony, mild irritation, and an inertia, a patience that borders on
resignation. We, the readers, arrive in cars headed toward that "trite, salt,
welcoming ocean," but only the emotional baggage we bring in the trunk
can transform this dreary New Jersey seascape into a world of completion
or closure. Of course, closure as such is not the point. Rather, the poem
attempts to engage or even seduce the reader, and it accomplishes this in
so low a key that it leaves us mildly frustrated, mildly engaged, and mildly
enlightened. And this lowering of register, lowering of intensity, and
lowering of expectation characterizes the "conversation poem" as we usually find it.

These three examples, as I have already conceded, by no means
convey the range of experiment in voice, diction, and rhetoric in contemporary poetry. The reaction against modernist impersonality is strong
but low-key for the most part. The legacies of Williams, Lowell, and
Stevens remain powerful motivating sources, but few younger poets seem
to have the aesthetic and intellectual range of their predecessors. The
rhetorical strategies developed in the first sixty years of this century are
taken for granted, but the need for them remains strong, and the rejection of certain formal techniques, despite the recent rise of the New
Formalists (whose rhetorical strategies remain colloquial and idiomatic)
still characterizes the stance of most living poets.

The rebellion against certain aspects of Eliot's (but not Pound's)
tradition-centered poetics remains especially strong, not so much because
of the conservative social views expressed in *After Strange Gods* but because of the social and political implications of his poetics. Politically self-
conscious, many younger poets worry that the withdrawal into cold individuality that characterizes the voice of the high modernist lyric-
monologue is inappropriate to our troubled, divided society. Whether
embracing the communal spirit without abandoning the romantic asser-

tion of individual being is entirely plausible, remains uncertain, and many attempts seem merely formulaic. And one might wonder if the attempt is worthwhile—whether, in fact, the impersonality of the modernist meditative poem isn't itself the perfect metaphor of the act of reading in a culture that no longer loves, trusts, or understands the poems it generates.

Works Cited

Ammons, A.R. 1981. *A Coast of Trees.* New York: Norton.

Ashbery, John. 1984. *A Wave.* New York: Viking-Penguin.

———. 1987. *April Galleons.* New York: Viking-Penguin.

Bates, Milton J. 1985. *Wallace Stevens: A Mythology of Self.* Berkeley: University of California Press.

Bergonzi, Bernard. 1978. *T.S. Eliot.* London: Macmillan.

Berryman, Jo Brentley. 1983. *Circe's Craft: Ezra Pound's* Hugh Selwyn Mauberley. Ann Arbor: UMI Research Press.

Bishop, Elizabeth. 1983. *The Complete Poems 1927–1979.* New York: Farrar, Straus and Giroux.

Bloom, Harold. 1976. *Figures of Capable Imagination.* New York: Seabury.

———. 1977. *Wallace Stevens: The Poems of Our Climate.* Ithaca, N.Y.: Cornell University Press.

———. 1988. *Poetics of Influence: New and Selected Criticism of Harold Bloom.* Ed. John Hollander. New Haven, Conn.: Henry R. Schwab.

Bloom, Harold, ed. 1987. *Modern Critical Views: Robert Lowell.* New York: Chelsea House.

Borroff, Marie. 1971. "Robert Frost's New Testament: Language and the Poem." *Modern Philology* 69.1:50–54.

Brower, Reuben A. 1963. *The Poetry of Robert Frost: Constellations of Intention.* New York: Oxford University Press.

Bush, Ronald. 1989. *The Genesis of Ezra Pound's* Cantos. 2nd ed. Princeton, N.J.: Princeton University Press.

Butler, Christopher. 1974. "Robert Lowell: From *Notebook* to *The Dolphin.*" *Yearbook of English Studies* 8:141–56.

Connolly, T. 1956. "Further Notes on Mauberley." *Accent* 16:59–67.

Cooper, John Xiros. 1987. *T.S. Eliot and the Politics of Voice: The Argument of* The Waste Land. Ann Arbor: UMI Research Press.

Costello, Bonnie. 1983. "'Polished Garlands of Agreeable Difference': William Carlos Williams and Marianne Moore, an Exchange." *The Motive for Metaphor: Essays on Modern Poetry.* Ed. Francis C. Bennington and Guy Rotella. Boston: Northeastern University Press. 64–81.

Culler, Jonathan. 1985. "Changes in the Study of the Lyric." *Lyric Poetry: Beyond New Criticism.* Ed. Chaviva Hošek and Patricia Parker. Ithaca, N.Y.: Cornell University Press. 38–54.

Deese, Helen. 1986. "Lowell and the Visual Arts." *Robert Lowell: Essays on the Poetry.* Ed. Stephen Axelrod and Helen Deese. New York: Cambridge University Press. 180–216.

De Man, Paul. 1984. *The Rhetoric of Romanticism.* New York: Columbia University Press.

D'Epiro, Peter. 1983. *A Loner of Rhetoric: Ezra Pound's Malatesta* Cantos. Ann Arbor: UMI Research Press.

Dugan, Alan. 1961. *Poems.* New Haven, Conn.: Yale University Press.

Eagleton, Terry. 1983. *Literary Theory: An Introduction.* Minneapolis: University of Minnesota Press.

Eliot, T.S. 1917. "Reflections on Contemporary Poetry." *The Egoist* 4.8:118–19; 4.10:151.

———. 1951. *Selected Essays.* London: Faber and Faber.

———. 1952. *The Complete Poems and Plays 1909–1950.* New York: Harcourt, Brace.

———. 1956. *The Frontiers of Criticism.* Minneapolis: University of Minnesota Press.

———. 1963. *Collected Poems 1909–1962.* New York: Harcourt, Brace and World.

Emerson, Ralph Waldo. 1983. *Essays and Lectures.* Ed. Joel Porte. New York: Library of America.

Espey, John J. 1955. *Ezra Pound's "Mauberley": A Study in Composition.* Berkeley: University of California Press.

Frost, Robert. 1964. *Selected Letters of Robert Frost.* Ed. Lawrance Thompson. New York: Holt, Rinehart and Winston.

———. 1966. *Selected Prose of Robert Frost.* Ed. Hyde Cox and Edward Connery Lathem. New York: Holt, Rinehart and Winston.

———. 1969. *The Poetry of Robert Frost.* Ed. Edward Connery Lathem. New York: Holt, Rinehart and Winston.

Glück, Louise. 1975. *The House on Marshland.* New York: Ecco.

———. 1990. *Ararat.* New York: Ecco.

Gray, Piers. 1982. *T.S. Eliot's Intellectual Development.* New York: Humanities.

Gruszewska-Wojtas, Ludmilla. 1988. "'The Street' and 'The Drawing Room': The Poetic Universe of T.S. Eliot's *Prufrock and Other Observations.*" *Essays in Poetics* 14.2:65–82.

Gusdorf, Georges. 1980. "Conditions and Limits of Autobiography." *Autobiography: Essays Theoretical and Critical.* Ed. James Olney. Princeton, N.J.: Princeton University Press. 28–48.

Hamilton, Ian. 1982. *Robert Lowell: A Biography.* New York: Random House.

Hartman, Geoffrey. 1980. *The Wilderness of Criticism.* New Haven, Conn.: Yale University Press.

Heaney, Seamus. 1980. "Robert Lowell: A Memorial Address Given at St. Luke's Church, Redcliffe Square, London, 5th October 1977." *Agenda* 18.3:23–33.

Holden, Jonathan. 1986. *Style and Authenticity in Postmodern Poetry.* Columbia: University of Missouri Press.

Jacobus, Mary. 1985. "Apostrophe and Lyric Voice in the *Prelude.*" *Lyric Poetry: Beyond New Criticism.* Ed. Chaviva Hošek and Patricia Parker. Ithaca, N.Y.: Cornell University Press. 167–81.

Jarrell, Randall. 1953a. "From the Kingdom of Necessity." *Poetry and the Age.* New York: Alfred A. Knopf. 188–99.

———. 1953b. "To the Laodiceans." *Poetry and the Age.* New York: Alfred A. Knopf. 37–69.

Johnson, W.R. 1982. *The Idea of Lyric: Lyric Modes in Ancient and Modern Poetry.* Berkeley: University of California Press.

Kenner, Hugh. 1971. *The Pound Era.* Berkeley: University of California Press.

———. 1987. *Ulysses.* 2nd ed. Baltimore: Johns Hopkins University Press.

Langbaum, Robert. 1983. "The Epiphanic Mode in Wordsworth and Modern Literature." *New Literary History* 14.2:335–58.

Lentricchia, Frank. 1975. *Robert Frost: Modern Poetics and the Landscapes of Self.* Durham, N.C.: Duke University Press.

———. 1980. *After the New Criticism.* Chicago: University of Chicago Press.

Lerner, Laurence. 1968. "Argument." *Princeton Encyclopedia of Poetry and Poetics.* Princeton, N.J.: Princeton University Press. 50.

Litz, A. Walton. 1973. "Introduction." *Eliot in His Time.* Princeton, N.J.: Princeton University Press.

Longenbach, James. 1987. *The Modernist Poetics of History.* Princeton, N.J.: Princeton University Press.

———. 1991. *Wallace Stevens: The Plain Sense of Things.* New York: Oxford University Press.

Lowell, Robert. 1959. *Life Studies.* New York: Farrar, Straus and Giroux.

———. 1964. *For the Union Dead.* New York: Farrar, Straus and Giroux.

———. 1967. *Near the Ocean.* New York: Farrar, Straus and Giroux.

———. 1969. *Notebook 1967–1968.* New York: Farrar, Straus and Giroux.

———. 1971. "A Conversation with Robert Lowell." Ian Hamilton, Interviewer. *The Review* 26:10–29.

———. 1973. *The Dolphin*. New York: Farrar, Straus and Giroux.

———. 1977a. *Day by Day*. New York: Farrar, Straus and Giroux.

———. 1977b. "After Enjoying Six or Seven Articles on Me." *Salmagundi* 37:112–15.

———. 1987. *Collected Prose*. New York: Farrar, Straus and Giroux.

———. Papers. Houghton Library, Harvard University.

Mahaffey, Vicki. 1969. "'The Death of Saint Narcissus' and 'Ode': Two Suppressed Poems by T.S. Eliot." *American Literature* 50.4:604–12.

Martin, Loy D. 1985. *Browning's Dramatic Monologue and the Post-Romantic Subject*. Baltimore: Johns Hopkins University Press.

Martz, Louis. 1963. "Introduction." *The Meditative Poem: An Anthology of Seventeenth-Century Verse*. Garden City, N.Y.: Doubleday.

Menand, Louis. 1987. *Discovering Modernism*. New York: Oxford University Press.

Moore, Marianne. 1924. *Observations*. New York: Dial.

———. 1986. *Complete Prose*. New York: Viking-Penguin.

Pinion, F.B. 1986. *A T.S. Eliot Companion*. London: Macmillan.

Pinsky, Robert. 1975. *Sadness and Happiness*. Princeton, N.J.: Princeton University Press.

———. 1976. *The Situation of Poetry*. Princeton, N.J.: Princeton University Press.

Poirier, Richard. 1977. *Robert Frost: The Work of Knowing*. New York: Oxford University Press.

Pound, Ezra. 1917a. "James Joyce, or At Last the Novel Appears." *The Egoist* 4.2:21–22.

———. 1917b. "Three Cantos." *Poetry* 10.3:113–21; 10.4:180–88; 10.5:248–54.

———. 1926. *Personae*. New York: Liveright.

———. 1950. *The Letters of Ezra Pound 1907–1941*. Ed. D.D. Paige. New York: Harcourt, Brace and World.

———. 1966. *Pound/Joyce: The Letters of Ezra Pound to James Joyce*. Ed. Forrest Reid. New York: New Directions.

———. 1973. *Selected Prose 1909–1965*. Ed. William Cookson. New York: New Directions.

———. Papers. Beinecke Library, Yale University.

———. Papers. Hamilton College Library.

Rajan, Tilottama. 1985. "Romanticism and the Death of Lyric Consciousness." *Lyric Poetry: Beyond New Criticism*. Ed. Chaviva Hošek and Patricia Parker. Ithaca, N.Y.: Cornell University Press. 194–207.

Rich, Adrienne. 1973. "Caryatid: A Column." *American Poetry Review* 2 (September-October 1973):42–43.

Said, Edward W. 1983. *The World, the Text, and the Critic*. Cambridge, Mass.: Harvard University Press.

Shusterman, Richard. 1989. "Aesthetic Education or Aesthetic Ideology: T.S. Eliot on Art's Moral Critique." *Philosophy and Literature* 13:96–114.

Smith, Grover. 1956. *T.S. Eliot's Poetry and Plays.* Chicago: University of Chicago Press.

Spanos, William V. 1965. "The Modulating Voice of Hugh Selwyn Mauberley." *Contemporary Literature* 6:73–96.

Stevens, Wallace. 1951. *The Necessary Angel.* New York: Alfred A. Knopf.

———. 1954. *Collected Poems.* New York: Alfred A.Knopf.

———. 1966. *Letters.* Ed. Holly Stevens. New York: Alfred A. Knopf.

———. 1984. *The Palm at the End of the Mind.* Ed. Holly Stevens. 2nd ed. Hamden, Conn.: Archon.

———. 1989a. *Opus Posthumous.* Ed. Milton J. Bates. New York: Alfred A. Knopf.

———. 1989b. *Sur Plusieurs Beaux Sujects: Wallace Stevens' Commonplace Book.* Ed. Milton J. Bates. Stanford: Stanford University Press.

Sukenick, Ronald. 1967. *Wallace Stevens: Musing the Obscure.* New York: New York University Press.

Sultan, Stanley. 1987. *Eliot, Joyce and Company.* New York: Oxford University Press.

Thoreau, Henry David. 1974. *The Maine Woods.* Princeton, N.J.: Princeton University Press.

Tucker, Herbert F. 1985. "Dramatic Monologue and the Overhearing of Lyric." *Lyric Poetry: Beyond New Criticism.* Ed. Chaviva Hošek and Patricia Parker. Ithaca, N.Y.: Cornell University Press. 226–43.

Vendler, Helen. 1969. *On Extended Wings: Wallace Stevens's Longer Poems.* Cambridge, Mass.: Harvard University Press.

———. 1984. *Wallace Stevens: Words Chosen Out of Desire.* Knoxville: University of Tennessee Press.

Volosinov, V.N. 1973. *Marxism and the Philosophy of Language.* Trans. Ladislav Matejka and I.R. Titunik. New York: Seminar.

Weaver, Mike. 1971. *William Carlos Williams: The American Background.* New York: Cambridge University Press.

Williams, William Carlos. 1925. *In the American Grain.* New York: Albert and Charles Boni. Rpt. New York: New Directions, 1956.

———. 1951. *Autobiography.* New York: Random House.

———. 1954. *Selected Essays.* New York: Random House.

———. 1957. *Selected Letters.* New York: McDowell, Oblensky.

———. 1958. *I Wanted to Write a Poem.* Boston: Beacon.

———. 1962. *Pictures from Brueghel.* New York: New Directions.

———. 1970. *Imaginations.* New York: New Directions.

———. 1986. *The Collected Poems of William Carlos Williams, Volume One: 1909–1939.* Ed. A. Walton Litz and Christopher MacGowan. New York: New Directions.

———. 1992. *Paterson*. Ed. Christopher MacGowan. Revised ed. New York: New Directions.

Williamson, Alan. 1984. *Introspection and Contemporary American Poetry.* Cambridge: Harvard University Press.

Yenser, Stephen. 1974. "Half-Legible Bronze?" *Poetry* 123.5:308–11.

Index